# Lean Lexicon

## A graphical glossary for Lean Thinkers

**Compiled by the Lean Enterprise Institute**
**Edited by Chet Marchwinski and John Shook**
**Foreword by Jose Ferro, Dan Jones, and Jim Womack**

The Lean Enterprise Institute
Cambridge, MA, USA
www.lean.org

Third Edition, Version 3.0
September 2006

With gratitude to Gary Berndt, Michael Brassard, Jon Carpenter, Mike Joyce, Dave LaHote, Dave Logozzo, Thomas Skehan, Art Smalley, Chuck Ward, and Helen Zak for their close review of the manuscript. The root cause of all remaining errors resides with the LEI senior advisors and editors.

# CONTENTS

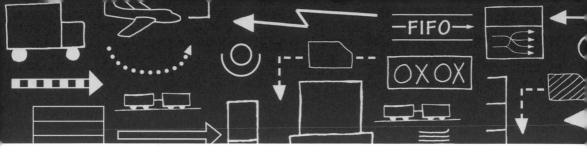

## FOREWORD

We receive many inquiries from members of the Lean Community asking for definitions of the terms we commonly use, ranging from *A3 report* to *yokoten*. In addition, as we attend events and visit companies we frequently find widespread confusion and inconsistent use of terms as simple and fundamental as *takt time*. (It's often still confused with *cycle time*.)

Chet Marchwinski, LEI's director of communications, and John Shook, an LEI senior advisor, have responded for several years now by clarifying many matters of terminology in response to individual requests and by placing these clarifications on the Community Page of the LEI web site. However, many Lean Thinkers continue to ask the meaning of lean terms and we have decided that the best course is simply to write them all down in one place in this *Lean Lexicon*. We have asked Chet and John, as veterans of the lean movement with broad knowledge of lean terminology at Toyota and elsewhere, to tackle this task.

Lexicon is just a fancy word for dictionary—one that conveniently alliterates with "lean"—and like all dictionaries, there is a need for upgrades as usage changes and new terms emerge. This is therefore Version 3.0 of what we imagine will be a continuing effort to define and sharpen our language as we all move toward future states and

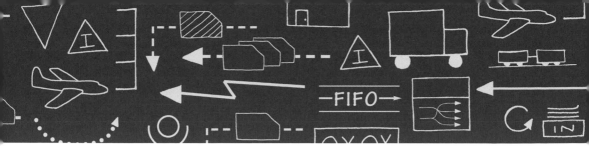

ideal states. In this spirit, we hope to hear from Lean Community members about additional terms to include in future versions and about changing usage and changing business needs that may call for revised definitions and additional examples.

As most Lean Thinkers know, precision is the key to lean performance: A precise *plan for every part*. Precisely determined *standardized work*. Precise *takt image* visible to everyone in a production process. Precise calculation of *standard inventory* at every point inventories still are needed. But to achieve precision on the *gemba* (see the definition on page 23) we require precision in our language. The *Lean Lexicon* is our effort to precisely meet this critical need.

Jose Ferro, Dan Jones, and Jim Womack
Sao Paulo, SP, Brazil
Ross-on-Wye, Herefordshire, UK
Cambridge, MA, USA

# INTRODUCTION

Drawing up a comprehensive list of lean terms is not an easy task. Many members of the Lean Community have gained their knowledge from different sources and use terms in slightly different ways. And many companies have developed their own "lean lingo" in an effort to customize usage to their needs and to make their production system unique. We therefore have devised two simple principles for selecting terms. These are:

1. The term is important.
   You really need it to successfully operate a lean system.
2. The term is in widespread use.
   It's not just "company speak," but lives in the broader community.

We also have needed to develop a common approach to definitions. As shown on the sample page at right, for each term we provide: A simple definition. An example, often showing different types of applications. Cross-references to related terms. An illustration, whenever possible. Of course, many terms, like *chief engineer* and *greenfield*, would be impossible to illustrate beyond photos of specific individuals and facilities!

As editors, we are acutely aware that there will be some differences within the Lean Community on definitions, and we have tried to provide the most common usage. We are even more aware that some important terms may have been left out. We therefore hope to hear suggestions for additions and improvements (which should be sent to: cmarchwinski@lean.org). We will post improvements on the Community Page of the LEI web site and issue revisions of the *Lean Lexicon* as appropriate.

Chet Marchwinski and John Shook
Bethel, CT, USA
Ann Arbor, MI, USA

**Term** ⟶ **Andon**
A visual management tool that highlights the status of the operations in an area at a single glance and that signals whenever an abnormality occurs.

**Definition** ⟶ An andon can indicate production status (for example, which machines are operating), an abnormality (for example, machine downtime, a quality problem, tooling faults, operator delays, and materials shortages), and needed actions, such as changeovers. An andon also can be used to display the status of production in terms of the number of units planned versus actual output.

**Example** ⟶ A typical andon, which is the Japanese term for "lamp," is an overhead signboard with rows of numbers corresponding to workstations or machines. A number lights when a problem is detected by a machine sensor, which automatically trips the appropriate light, or by an operator who pulls a cord or pushes a button. The illuminated number summons a quick response from the team leader. Colored lighting on top of machines to signal problems (red) or normal operations (green) is another type of andon.

**Cross-reference** ⟶ *See*: Jidoka, Visual Management.

**Illustration** ⟶

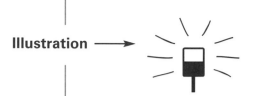

Simple andon.

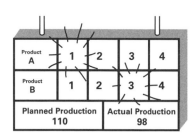

Complex andon.

3

## Third Edition Highlights

- Genchi Genbutsu
- Group Leaders
- Hansei
- Isolated Islands
- Jishuken
- Lean Consumption
- Lean Consumption Maps
- Lean Provision Maps
- Lean Provision
- Preventive Maintenance
- Quality Control Circle
- Quality Function Deployment (QFD)
- Resident Engineer
- Shojinka
- Six Sigma
- Team Leader
- Theory of Constraints (TOC)
- Total Quality Control (TQC)
- Total Quality Management
- Work Element
- Yokoten

## Treatment of Foreign Terms

Our editorial North Star, *The Chicago Manual of Style*, states that foreign words usually are set in italics if they are likely to be unfamiliar to readers. And in many works on lean production and lean thinking terms such as *kaizen* and *muda* are italicized. However, in preparing this lexicon, our objective is to bring all of these terms into common usage. Plus, we have no way to know which terms are now familiar and which are still novel across the Lean Community.

We therefore have decided to welcome the entire list of terms into the English language and have set all of them in plain type. To avoid any confusion, we have included a list of all foreign words in Appendix C so readers may be sure of each term's point of origin.

# A3 Report

A Toyota-pioneered practice of getting the problem, the analysis, the corrective actions, and the action plan down on a single sheet of large (A3) paper, often with the use of graphics. At Toyota, A3 reports have evolved into a standard method for summarizing problem-solving exercises, status reports, and planning exercises like value-stream mapping.

A3 paper is the international term for paper 297 millimeters wide and 420 millimeters long. The closest U.S. paper size is the 11-by-17 inch tabloid sheet.

*See:* Value-Stream Mapping (VSM).

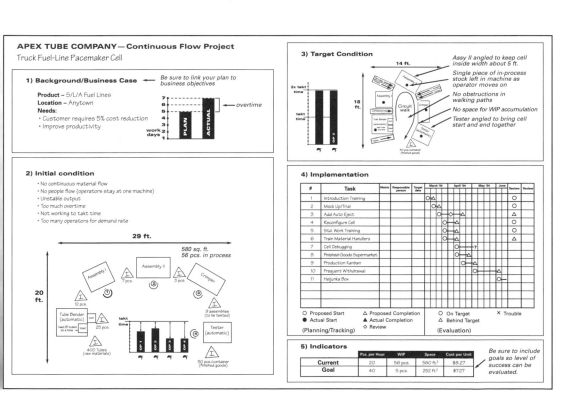

## A-B Control

A way to regulate the working relationships between two machines or operations to control overproduction and ensure balanced use of resources.

In the Illustration, neither of the machines nor the conveyor will cycle unless three conditions are met: Machine A is full, the conveyor contains the standard amount of work-in-process (in this case, one piece), and Machine B is empty. When those conditions are met, all three will cycle once and wait until the conditions are met again.

*See:* Inventory, Overproduction.

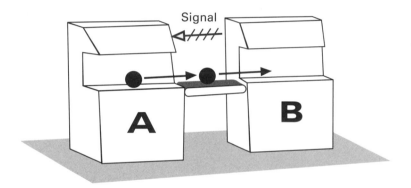

Signal

## ABC Production Analysis

Segmenting part numbers into groups based on demand. Lean Thinkers use this analysis to decide how much and for which products to hold inventory. A items are high runners, B items are medium runners, and C items are low runners. C items typically include infrequent color and build combinations, special-edition items, and replacement parts.

*See:* Flow Production, Pull Production.

## Andon

A visual management tool that highlights the status of operations in an area at a single glance and that signals whenever an abnormality occurs.

An andon can indicate production status (for example, which machines are operating), an abnormality (for example, machine downtime, a quality problem, tooling faults, operator delays, and materials shortages), and needed actions, such as changeovers. An andon also can be used to display the status of production in terms of the number of units planned versus actual output.

A typical andon, which is the Japanese term for "lamp," is an overhead signboard with rows of numbers corresponding to workstations or machines. A number lights when a problem is detected by a machine sensor, which automatically trips the appropriate light, or by an operator who pulls a cord or pushes a button. The illuminated number summons a quick response from the team leader. Colored lighting on top of machines to signal problems (red) or normal operations (green) is another type of andon.

*See:* Jidoka, Visual Management.

Simple andon.

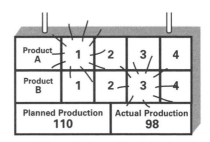

Complex andon.

## Automatic Line Stop

Ensuring that a production process stops whenever a problem or defect occurs.

For an automated line this usually involves the installation of sensors and switches that automatically stop the line when an abnormality is detected. For a manual line a fixed-position stop system often is installed. This permits operators to pull an overhead cord or push a button that stops the process at the end of a work cycle if the problem encountered cannot be fixed during the cycle.

These examples illustrate the lean principle of jidoka, which prevents defects from going to the next phase of production and avoids the waste of making a series of defective items. Mass producers, by contrast, will try to keep lines running to achieve high equipment utilization, even when known defects occur repetitively and require rework at the end of the process.

*See:* Error-Proofing, Fixed-Position Stop System, Jidoka.

Automatic line stop.

## Autonomation
*See:* Jidoka.

Batch-and-queue production.

## Batch-and-Queue
A mass production approach to operations in which large lots (batches) of items are processed and moved to the next process—regardless of whether they are actually needed—where they wait in a line (a queue).

*See:* Continuous Flow, Lean Production, Overproduction, Push Production.

## Brownfield
An existing production facility, usually managed in accordance with mass production thinking.
*Compare:* Greenfield.

## Buffer Stock
*See:* Inventory.

## Building in Quality, Built-in Quality
*See:* Jidoka.

## Build-to-Order
A situation in which production lead time and order lead time are less than the time the customer is prepared to wait for the product, and the producer builds products entirely to confirmed order rather than to forecast.

This is a condition Lean Thinkers strive to achieve because it avoids the demand amplification and waste inherently involved in building products based on informed guesses about customer desires.

*See:* Demand Amplification, Heijunka, Level Selling.

## Capital Linearity

A philosophy for designing and buying production machinery so that small amounts of capacity can be added or subtracted as demand changes. In this way, the amount of capital needed per part produced can be very nearly level (linear).

For example, in capacitizing for 100,000 units of annual output, a manufacturer might purchase a series of machines, each with an annual capacity of 100,000 units, and link them in one continuous flow production line (first alternative). Alternatively, the manufacturer might buy 10 sets of smaller machines to install in 10 cells, with each cell having annual capacity of 10,000 units (second alternative).

If the forecast of 100,000 units proved to be exactly correct, the single line with 100,000 units might be the most capital efficient. But if real demand is different, the second alternative offers distinct advantages:

- Whenever demand goes beyond 100,000 units, the manufacturer can add either another line with 100,000 units of capacity or just the required number of cells, each with 10,000 units of capacity, to satisfy the higher demand. By adding cells, the capital investment per unit of output would vary only slightly with changing demand. It would be very nearly linear.

Whenever the real demand is less than 100,000 units, a more serious problem arises. The first alternative makes it almost impossible to decrease capacity and maintain efficiency at the current level. However, the second alternative allows the manufacturer to subtract capacity by shutting down as many cells as required.

*See:* Labor Linearity, Monument, Right-Sized Tools.

## Catchball

*See:* Policy Deployment.

## Cell

The location of processing steps for a product immediately adjacent to each other so that parts, documents, etc., can be processed in very nearly continuous flow, either one at a time or in small batch sizes that are maintained through the complete sequence of processing steps.

A U shape (shown below) is common because it minimizes walking distance and allows different combinations of work tasks for operators. This is an important consideration in lean production because the number of operators in a cell will change with changes in demand. A U shape also facilitates performance of the first and last steps in the process by the same operator, which is helpful in maintaining work pace and smooth flow.

Many companies use the terms *cell* and *line* interchangeably.

There is a school of thought that material should flow through cells in a right-to-left direction relative to the operator, because more people are right handed and it is more efficient and natural to work from right to left. However, many efficient processes flow to the left and many flow to the right. Simply evaluate on a case-by-case basis whether a particular direction makes more sense.

*See:* Continuous Flow, Operator Balance Chart, Standardized Work.

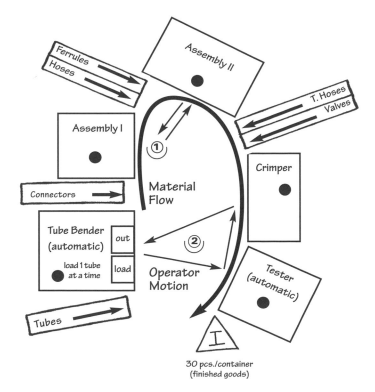

Example of a U-shaped cell.

## Chaku-Chaku

A method of conducting one-piece flow in a cell where machines unload parts automatically so that the operator (or operators) can carry a part directly from one machine to the next without stopping to unload the part, thus saving time and motion.

For instance, the first machine in a processing sequence automatically ejects a part as soon as its cycle is completed. The operator takes the part to the next machine in the sequence, which has just finished cycling and ejected its part. The operator loads the new part, starts the machine, and takes the ejected part to the next machine, which has just finished cycling and ejected its part and so on around the cell. The term literally means "load-load" in Japanese.

*See:* Cell, Continuous Flow.

## Change Agent

The leader of a lean conversion who has the willpower and drive to initiate fundamental change and make it stick.

The change agent—who often comes from outside the organization —doesn't need detailed lean knowledge at the beginning of the conversion. The knowledge can come from a lean expert, but the change agent absolutely needs the will to see that the knowledge is applied and becomes the new way of working.

*Compare:* Sensei.

## Changeover

The process of switching from the production of one product or part number to another in a machine (e.g., a stamping press or molding machine) or a series of linked machines (e.g., an assembly line or cell) by changing parts, dies, molds, fixtures, etc. (Also called a *setup*.) Changeover time is measured as the time elapsed between the last piece in the run just completed and the first good piece from the process after the changeover.

*See:* Single Minute Exchange of Die (SMED).

## Chief Engineer

The term used at Toyota for the manager with total responsibility for the development and success of a product line (a car platform or a major variant developed from a platform). The chief engineer (previously known by the Japanese term shusa) leads the development process from the beginning of product development into production. When the lessons learned are summarized, the chief engineer begins the development cycle for the next generation. The chief engineer's responsibility extends to the market share and profitability of the product.

Chief engineers typically have deep engineering skills but little staff. They coordinate rather than directly control employees assigned to programs from functional areas such as body engineering, drivetrain engineering, and purchasing.

*See:* Value-Stream Manager.

## Continuous Flow

Producing and moving one item at a time (or a small and consistent batch of items) through a series of processing steps as continuously as possible, with each step making just what is requested by the next step.

Continuous flow can be achieved in a number of ways, ranging from moving assembly lines to manual cells. It also is called *one-piece flow*, *single-piece flow*, and *make one, move one*.

*See:* Batch-and-Queue, Flow Production, One-Piece Flow.

Continuous flow processing.

## Cross-Dock

A facility that sorts and recombines a variety of inbound items from many suppliers for outbound shipment to many customers, such as assembly plants, distributors, or retailers.

A common example is a facility operated by a manufacturer with many plants in order to efficiently gather materials from many suppliers. When a truck loaded with pallets of goods from suppliers arrives on one side of the dock, the pallets are immediately unloaded, and taken to several shipping lanes for loading onto outbound trucks bound for different facilities.

A cross-dock is not a warehouse because it does not store goods. Instead, goods are usually unloaded from inbound vehicles and moved to shipping lanes for outbound vehicles in one step. If outbound vehicles leave frequently, it may be possible to clear the floor of the cross-dock every 24 hours.

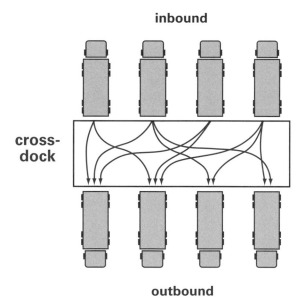

## Current-State Map
*See:* Value-Stream Mapping (VSM).

## Cycle Time
How often a part or product is completed by a process, as timed by observation. This time includes operating time plus the time required to prepare, load, and unload.

The appropriate calculation of cycle time may depend upon context. For example, if a paint process completes a batch of 22 parts every five minutes, the cycle time for the batch is five minutes. However, the cycle time for an individual part is 13.6 seconds (5 minutes x 60 seconds = 300 seconds, divided by 22 parts = 13.6 seconds).

## Cycle Time — Related Terms Involving Time
### Effective Machine Cycle Time
*Machine cycle time* plus load and unload time, plus the result of dividing changeover time by the number of pieces between changeovers. For example, if a machine has a cycle time of 20 seconds, plus a combined load and unload time of 30 seconds, and a changeover time of 30 seconds divided by a minimum batch size of 30, the Effective Machine Cycle Time is 20+30+(30/30) or 1 = 51 seconds.

### Machine Cycle Time
The time a machine requires to complete all of its operations on one piece.

### Nonvalue-Creating Time
The time spent on activities that add costs but no value to an item from the customer's perspective. Such activities typically include storage, inspection, and rework.

### Operator Cycle Time
The time it takes an operator to complete all the work elements at a station before repeating them, as timed by direct observation.

### Order Lead Time
*Production lead time* plus time expended downstream in getting the product to the customer, including delays for processing orders and entering them into production and delays when customer orders exceed production capacity. In other words, the time the customer must wait for the product.

### Order-to-Cash Time
The amount of time that elapses from the receipt of a customer order until the producer receives cash payment from the customer. This can be more or less than *order lead time*, depending on whether a producer is in a build-to-order or a ship-from-stock mode, on terms of payment, etc.

### Processing Time
The time a product actually is being worked on in design or production and the time an order actually is being processed. Typically, processing time is a small fraction of *production lead time*.

### Production Lead Time (also Throughput Time and Total Product Cycle Time)
The time required for a product to move all the way through a process or a value stream from start to finish. At the plant level this often is termed door-to-door time. The concept also can be applied to the time required for a design to progress from start to finish in product development or for a product to proceed from raw materials all the way to the customer.

### Value-Creating Time
The time of those work elements that actually transform the product in a way that the customer is willing to pay for. Usually, value-creating time is less than *cycle time*, which is less than *production lead time*.

*See:* Value.

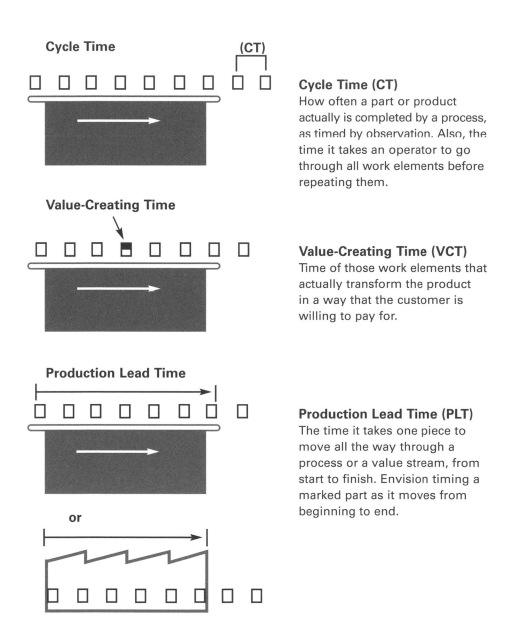

**Cycle Time**

**(CT)**

## Cycle Time (CT)
How often a part or product actually is completed by a process, as timed by observation. Also, the time it takes an operator to go through all work elements before repeating them.

**Value-Creating Time**

## Value-Creating Time (VCT)
Time of those work elements that actually transform the product in a way that the customer is willing to pay for.

**Production Lead Time**

## Production Lead Time (PLT)
The time it takes one piece to move all the way through a process or a value stream, from start to finish. Envision timing a marked part as it moves from beginning to end.

**or**

**Usually: VCT < CT < PLT**

## Demand Amplification

The tendency in any multistage process for production orders received by each upstream process to be more erratic than actual production or sales at the next downstream process. This also is called the *Forrester Effect* (after Jay Forrester at MIT who first characterized this phenomenon mathematically in the 1950s) and the *Bullwhip Effect*.

The two main causes of demand amplification as orders move upstream are: (a) The number of decision points where orders can be adjusted; and (b) delays while orders wait to be processed and passed on (such as waiting for the weekly run of the Material Requirements Planning system). The longer the delays, the greater the amplification as more production is determined by forecasts (which become less accurate the longer the forecasting horizon) and as more adjustments are made to the orders (by system algorithms adding "just-in-case" amounts).

Lean Thinkers strive to use leveled pull systems with frequent withdrawals for production and shipping instructions at each stage of the value stream in order to minimize demand amplification.

The demand amplification chart below shows a typical situation in which the variation in demand at the customer end of the value stream (Alpha) is modest, about +/-3% during a month. But as orders travel back up the value stream through Beta and Gamma they become very erratic until Gamma's orders sent to its raw materials supplier vary by +/-35% during a month.

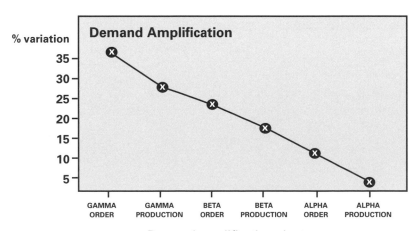

Demand amplification chart.

The demand amplification chart is an excellent way to raise consciousness about the degree of amplification present in a production system. If demand amplification could be completely eliminated, the variation in orders at every point along this value stream would be +/-3%, reflecting the true variation in customer demand.

*See:* Build-to-Order, Heijunka, Level Selling.


## Design-In

Collaboration between a customer and a supplier to design both a component and its manufacturing process.

Typically the customer provides cost and performance targets (sometimes called an *envelope*) with the supplier doing detailed design of the component and manufacturing process (tooling, layout, quality, etc.). The supplier often stations a resident engineer at the customer to ensure that the component will work properly with the completed product to minimize total cost.

Design-in contrasts with *work-to-print* approaches in which the supplier simply is given a complete design and told to tool and produce it.

*See:* Resident Engineer.


## Downtime

Production time lost due to planned or unplanned stoppages.

Planned downtime includes scheduled stoppages for activities such as beginning-of-the-shift production meetings, changeovers to produce other products, and scheduled maintenance.

Unplanned downtime includes stoppages for breakdowns, machine adjustments, materials shortages, and absenteeism.

*See:* Overall Equipment Effectiveness, Total Productive Maintenance.

## Efficiency

Meeting exact customer requirements with the minimum amount of resources.

### Apparent Efficiency vs. True Efficiency

Taiichi Ohno illustrated the common confusion between *apparent efficiency* and *true efficiency* with an example of 10 people producing 100 units daily. If improvements to the process boost output to 120 units daily, there is an apparent 20 percent gain in efficiency. But this is true only if demand also increases by 20 percent. If demand remains stable at 100 the only way to increase the efficiency of the process is to figure out how to produce the same number of units with less effort and capital. (Ohno 1988, p. 61.)

### Total Efficiency vs. Local Efficiency

Toyota also commonly distinguishes between *total efficiency*, involving the performance of an entire production process or value stream, and *local efficiency*, involving the performance of one point or step within a production process or value stream. It emphasizes achieving efficiency in the former over the latter.

*See:* Overproduction, Seven Wastes.

Current state — 10 operators          **100 pieces**

"But I only need 100 pieces!"

Apparent efficiency — 10 operators          **120 pieces**

customer

True efficiency — 8 operators          **100 pieces**

## Error-Proofing

Methods that help operators avoid mistakes in their work caused by choosing the wrong part, leaving out a part, installing a part backwards, etc. Also called *mistake-proofing*, *poka-yoke* (error-proofing) and *baka-yoke* (fool-proofing).

Common examples of error-proofing include:

- Product designs with physical shapes that make it impossible to install parts in any but the correct orientation.

- Photocells above parts containers to prevent a product from moving to the next stage if the operator's hands have not broken the light to obtain necessary parts.

- A more complex parts monitoring system, again using photocells, but with additional logic to make sure the right combination of parts was selected for the specific product being assembled.

*See:* Inspection, Jidoka.

A contact-type error-proofing device.

## Every Product Every Interval (EPEx)

The frequency with which different part numbers are produced in a production process or system.

If a machine is changed over in a sequence so that every part number assigned to it is produced every three days, then EPEx is three days. In general, it is good for EPEx to be as small as possible in order to produce small lots of each part number and minimize inventories in the system. However, a machine's EPEx will depend on changeover times and the number of part numbers assigned to the machine. A machine with long changeovers (and large minimum batch sizes) running many part numbers will inevitably have a large EPEx unless changeover times or the number of part numbers can be reduced.

*See:* Heijunka.

## Fill-Up System

A *pull production* system in which preceding (supplier) processes produce only enough to replace—or fill up—product withdrawn by following (customer) processes.

*See:* Kanban, Pull Production, Supermarket.

## First In, First Out (FIFO)

The principle and practice of maintaining precise production and conveyance sequence by ensuring that the first part to enter a process or storage location is also the first part to exit. (This ensures that stored parts do not become obsolete and that quality problems are not buried in inventory.) FIFO is a necessary condition for pull system implementation.

The FIFO sequence often is maintained by a painted lane or physical channel that holds a certain amount of inventory. The supplying process fills the lane from the upstream end while the customer process withdraws from the downstream end. If the lane fills up, the supplying process must stop producing until the customer consumes some of the inventory. This way the FIFO lane can prevent the supplying process from overproducing even though the supplying process is not linked to the consuming process by continuous flow or a supermarket.

FIFO is one way to regulate a pull system between two decoupled processes when it is not practical to maintain an inventory of all possible part variations in a supermarket because the parts are one-of-a-kind, have short shelf lives, or are very expensive but required infrequently. In this application, the removal of the one part in a FIFO lane by the consuming process automatically triggers the production of one additional part by the supplying process.

*See:* Kanban, Pull Production, Supermarket.

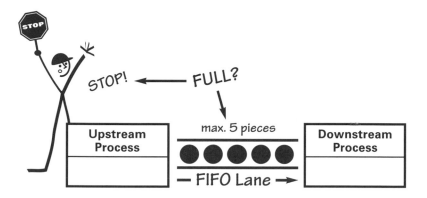

An example of a FIFO lane with five pieces in the lane.

## Five Ss

Five related terms, beginning with an *S* sound, describing workplace practices conducive to visual control and lean production. The five terms in Japanese are:

1. **Seiri**: Separate needed from unneeded items—tools, parts, materials, paperwork—and discard the unneeded.

2. **Seiton**: Neatly arrange what is left—a place for everything and everything in its place.

3. **Seiso**: Clean and wash.

4. **Seiketsu**: Cleanliness resulting from regular performance of the first three Ss.

5. **Shitsuke**: Discipline, to perform the first four Ss.

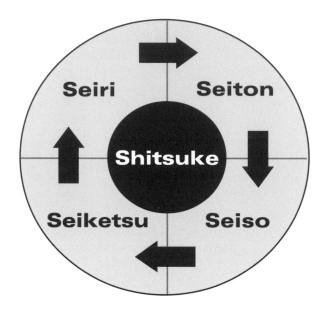

The Five Ss often are translated into English as Sort, Straighten, Shine, Standardize, and Sustain. Some lean practitioners add a sixth S for Safety: Establish and practice safety procedures in the workshop and office. However, Toyota traditionally refers to just Four Ss:

1. **Sifting** (Seiri): Go through everything in the work area, separating and eliminating what isn't needed.

2. **Sorting** (Seiton): Arrange items that are needed in a neat and easy-to-use manner.

3. **Sweeping Clean** (Seiso): Clean up the work area, equipment, and tools.

4. **Spic and Span** (Seiketsu): The overall cleanliness and order that result from disciplined practice of the first three Ss.

The last S — shitsuke (sustain) — is dropped because it becomes redundant under Toyota's system of daily, weekly, and monthly audits to check standardized work. Whether four, five, or six Ss are used, the key point to remember is that the effort is systematic and organic to lean production, not a "bolt-on" stand-alone program.

*See:* Standardized Work.

## Five Whys

The practice of asking *why* repeatedly whenever a problem is encountered in order to get beyond the obvious symptoms to discover the root cause.

For instance, Taiichi Ohno gives this example about a machine that stopped working (Ohno 1988, p. 17):

1. Why did the machine stop?
   There was an overload and the fuse blew.

2. Why was there an overload?
   The bearing was not sufficiently lubricated.

3. Why was it not lubricated?
   The lubrication pump was not pumping sufficiently.

4. Why was it not pumping sufficiently?
   The shaft of the pump was worn and rattling.

5. Why was the shaft worn out?
   There was no strainer attached and metal scraps got in.

Without repeatedly asking why, managers would simply replace the fuse or pump and the failure would recur. The specific number *five* is not the point. Rather it is to keep asking until the root cause is reached and eliminated.

*See:* Kaizen; Plan, Do, Check, Act (PDCA).

## Fixed-Position Stop System

A method of addressing problems on assembly lines by stopping the line at the end of the work cycle—that is, at a fixed position—if a problem is detected that cannot be solved during the work cycle.

In the fixed-position stop system, an operator discovering a problem with parts, tools, materials supply, safety conditions, etc., pulls a rope or pushes a button to signal the supervisor. The supervisor assesses the situation and determines if the problem can be fixed before the end of the current work cycle. If the problem can be fixed, the supervisor resets the signal system so the line doesn't stop. If the problem can't be corrected within the remainder of the cycle time, the line stops at the end of the work cycle.

The fixed-position stop system was pioneered by Toyota to solve three problems: (1) The reluctance of production associates to pull the signal cord if the entire line would be stopped immediately; (2) unnecessary line stoppages to deal with minor problems that could be resolved within one work cycle; and (3) the need to stop the line at the end of a work cycle rather than mid-way through the cycle to avoid the confusion—plus the quality and safety problems—inherent in restarting work tasks part of the way through a cycle.

The fixed-position stop system is a method of jidoka, or building in quality, on manual processes along moving assembly lines.

*See:* Andon, Automatic Line Stop, Jidoka.

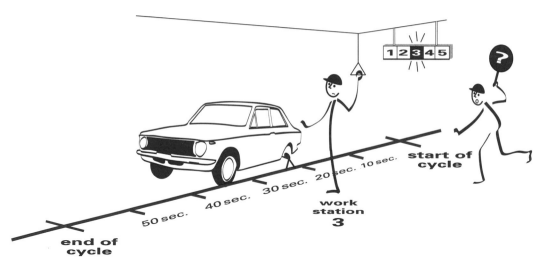

Fixed-position stop system.

## Flow Production

The production system Henry Ford introduced at his Highland Park, MI, plant in 1913.

The objective of flow production was to drastically reduce product throughput time and human effort through a series of innovations.

These included consistently interchangeable parts so that cycle times could be stable for every job along an extended line, the line itself, the reconfiguration of part fabrication tasks so that machines were lined up in process sequence with parts flowing quickly and smoothly from machine to machine, and a production control system insuring that the production rate in parts fabrication matched the consumption rate of parts in final assembly.

*See:* Continuous Flow.
*Compare:* Mass Production.

## Four Ms
The variables that a production system manipulates to produce value for customers. The first three are resources, the fourth is the way the resources are used. In a lean system, the Four Ms mean:

1. **Material**—no defects or shortages.

2. **Machine**—no breakdowns, defects, or unplanned stoppages.

3. **Man**—good work habits, necessary skills, punctuality, and no unscheduled absenteeism.

4. **Method**—standardized processes, maintenance, and management.

## Future-State Map
*See:* Value-Stream Mapping (VSM).

## Gemba
The Japanese term for "actual place," often used for the shop floor or any place where value-creating work actually occurs.

The term often is used to stress that real improvement only can take place when there is a shop-floor focus based on direct observation of current conditions where work is done. For example, standardized work cannot be written down at a desk in the engineering office, but must be defined and revised on the gemba.

### Genchi Genbutsu

The Toyota practice of thoroughly understanding a condition by confirming information or data through personal observation at the source of the condition.

For example, a decision maker investigating a problem will go to the shop floor to observe the process being investigated and interact with workers to confirm data and understand the situation, rather than relying solely on computer data or information from others. The practice applies to executives as well as managers. In Japanese, genchi genbutsu essentially means "go and see" but translates directly as "actual place and actual thing."

*See*: Gemba.

### Greenfield

A new production facility providing the opportunity to introduce lean working methods in a new work culture where the inertia of the past is not a barrier.

*Compare:* Brownfield.

### Group Leaders

At Toyota, these are the front-line supervisors who typically lead a group of four teams or 20 workers; called kumicho in Japanese.

A group leader's duties, among others, include planning production, reporting results, coordinating improvement activities, scheduling vacation and manpower, developing team members, testing process changes, and performing daily audits of team leaders to make sure they have done their standard work audits of team members. They also do a weekly Five S audit of their teams' work areas.

*See*: Five Ss, Team Leader.

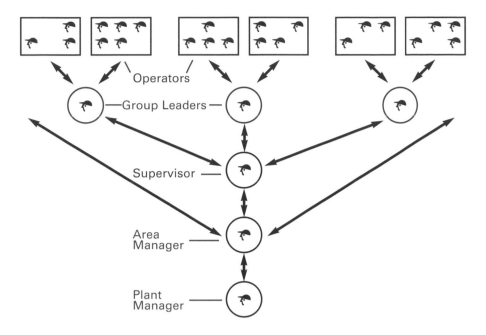

Location of group leaders in typical chain of responsibility.

## Hansei

The continuous improvement practice of looking back and thinking about how a process or personal shortcoming can be improved; the Japanese term for "self-reflection."

In the Toyota Production System, hansei or reflection meetings typically are held at key milestones and at the end of a project to identify problems, develop countermeasures, and communicate the improvements to the rest of the organization so mistakes aren't repeated. Thus, hansei is a critical part of organizational learning along with kaizen and standardized work. It sometimes is compared to "check" in the plan-do-check-act improvement cycle.

*See*: Kaizen; Plan, Do, Check, Act; Standardized Work; Toyota Production System (TPS).

## Heijunka

Leveling the type and quantity of production over a fixed period of time. This enables production to efficiently meet customer demands while avoiding batching and results in minimum inventories, capital costs, manpower, and production lead time through the whole value stream.

With regard to level production by quantity of items, suppose that a producer routinely received orders for 500 items per week, but with significant variation by day: 200 arrive on Monday, 100 on Tuesday, 50 on Wednesday, 100 on Thursday, and 50 on Friday. To level production, the producer might place a small buffer of finished goods near shipping, to respond to Monday's high level of demand, and level production at 100 units per day through the week. By keeping a small stock of finished goods at the very end of the value stream, this producer can level demand to its plant and to its suppliers, making for more efficient utilization of assets along the entire value stream while meeting customer requirements.

With regard to leveling production by type of item, as illustrated on the next page, suppose that a shirt company offers Models A, B, C, and D to the public and that weekly demand for shirts is five of Model A, three of Model B, and two each of Models C and D. A mass producer, seeking economies of scale and wishing to minimize changeovers between products, would probably build these products in the weekly sequence **A A A A A B B B C C D D**.

A lean producer, mindful—in addition to the benefits outlined above—of the effect of sending large, infrequent batches of orders upstream to suppliers, would strive to build in the repeating sequence **A A B C D A A B C D A B**, making appropriate production system improvements, such as reducing changeover times. This sequence would be adjusted periodically according to changing customer orders.

In Japanese, the word heijunka means, roughly, "levelization."

*See:* Demand Amplification, Every Product Every Interval (EPEx), Just-in-Time (JIT), Muda, Mura, Muri, SMED.

## Heijunka by Product Type

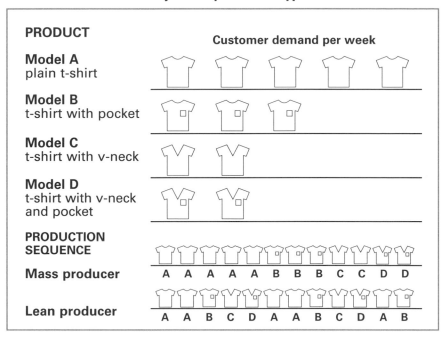

(Note that this example does not address heijunka by production quantity.)

## Heijunka Box

A tool used to level the mix and volume of production by distributing kanban within a facility at fixed intervals. Also called a leveling box.

In the illustration (on the next page) of a typical heijunka box, each horizontal row is for one type of product (one part number). Each vertical column represents identical time intervals for paced withdrawal of kanban. The shift starts at 7:00 a.m. and the kanban withdrawal interval is every 20 minutes. This is the frequency with which the material handler withdraws kanban from the box and distributes them to production processes in the facility.

Whereas the slots represent the material and information flow timing, the kanban in the slots each represent one *pitch* of production for one product type. (Pitch is the takt time multiplied by the pack-out quantity.) In the case of Product A, the pitch is 20 minutes and there is one kanban in the slot for each time interval. However, the pitch for Product B is 10 minutes, so there are two kanban in each slot. Product C has a pitch of 40 minutes, so there are kanban in every other slot. Products D and E share a production process with a pitch of 20 minutes and a ratio of demand for Product D versus Product E of 2:1. Therefore, there is a kanban for Product D in the first two intervals of the shift and a kanban for Product E in the third interval, and so on in the same sequence.

Used as illustrated, the heijunka box consistently levels demand by short time increments (instead of releasing a shift, day, or week's worth of demand to the floor) and levels demand by mix (for example, by ensuring that Product D and Product E are produced in a steady ratio with small batch sizes).

*See:* Every Product Every Interval (EPEx), Heijunka, Kanban, Material Handling, Paced Withdrawal, Pitch.

## Heijunka Box

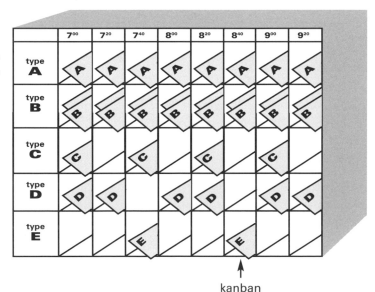

one row per product type

kanban

**Hoshin Kanri**
*See:* Policy Deployment.


**Ideal-State Map**
*See:* Value-Stream Mapping (VSM).


**Information Flow**
The movement of information on customer desires backward from the customer to the points where the information is needed to direct each operation.

In companies based on mass production principles, the flow of information usually takes parallel forms: Forecasts flowing back from company to company and facility to facility; schedules flowing back from company to company and facility to facility; daily (or weekly or hourly) shipping orders telling each facility what to ship on the next shipment; and expedited information countermanding forecasts, schedules, and shipping orders to adjust the production system to changing conditions.

Companies applying Lean Thinking try to simplify information flows by establishing a single scheduling point for production and instituting *pull loops* of information. These go upstream to the previous production point and from that point to the previous point—all the way to the earliest production point.

The illustrations (on the next page) show the multiple paths for information flows in mass production compared with the simpler flows in lean production. Note that lean producers still provide forecasts, because firms and facilities further from the customer need advance notice to plan capacity, schedule their workforce, calculate takt time, adjust for seasonal variations, introduce new models, and so forth. However, the day-to-day flow of production information can be compressed from schedules, shipping releases, and expediting to simple pull loops.

*See:* Value-Stream Mapping (VSM).

## Current-State Information Flow in Mass Production

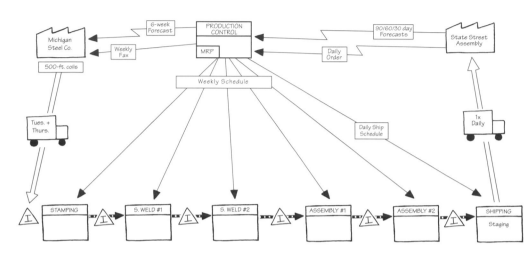

## Future-State Information Flow in Lean Production

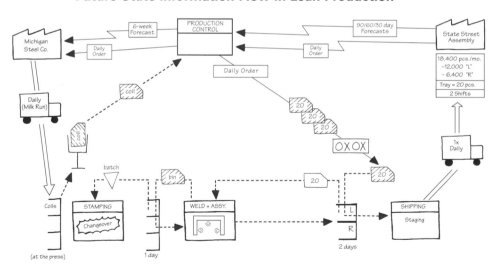

Information flows are shown in blue. Map symbols on
information flow are explained in Appendix A.

## Inspection

In mass production, the practice of quality checking products by specialized inspectors outside of the process making the products.

Lean producers assign quality assurance to operators and mistake-proofing devices within the production process in order to detect problems at the source. Rather than passing defects to subsequent processes for detection and rectification, the process is stopped to determine the cause and to take corrective action.

*See:* Error-Proofing, Jidoka.


## Inventory

Materials (and information) present along a value stream between processing steps.

Physical inventories usually are categorized by position in the value stream and by purpose. *Raw materials, work-in-process*, and *finished goods* are terms used to describe the position of the inventory within the production process. *Buffer stocks*, *safety stocks*, and *shipping stocks* are terms used to describe the purpose of the inventory. Since inventory always has both a position and a purpose (and some inventories have more than one purpose) the same items may be, for example, finished goods and buffer stocks. Similarly, the same items may be raw materials and safety stocks. And some items even may be finished goods, buffer stocks, and safety stocks (particularly if the value stream between raw materials and finished goods is short).

The size of the buffer and safety inventory levels will depend on the amplitude of the variations in downstream demand (creating the need for buffer stock) and the capability of the upstream process (creating the need for safety stock). Good lean practice is to determine the inventory for a process and to continually reduce it when possible, but only after reducing downstream variability and increasing upstream capability. Lowering inventory without addressing variability or capability will only disappoint the customer as the process fails to deliver needed products on time.

To avoid confusion, it is important to define each type of inventory carefully.

### Buffer Stock
Goods held, usually at the downstream end of a facility or process, to protect the customer from starvation in the event of an abrupt increase in short-term demand that exceeds short-term production capacity.

The terms buffer and safety stock often are used interchangeably, which creates confusion. There is an important difference between the two, which can be summarized as: Buffer stock protects your customer from you (the producer) in the event of an abrupt demand change; safety stock protects you from incapability in your upstream processes and your suppliers.

### Finished Goods
Items a facility has completed that await shipment.

### Raw Materials
Goods in a facility that have not yet been processed.

### Safety Stock
Goods held at any point (raw materials, WIP, or finished goods) to prevent downstream customers from being starved by upstream process capability issues. Also called emergency stock.

### Shipping Stock
Goods in shipping lanes at the downstream end of a facility that are being built up for the next shipment. (These generally are proportional to shipping batch sizes and frequencies.) Also called cycle stock.

Inventories categorized by position in the value stream

Inventories categorized by purpose

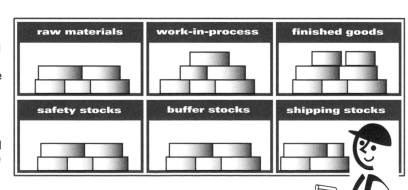

The six types of inventory.

## Work-in-Process (WIP)

Items between processing steps within a facility. In lean systems, standardized work-in-process is the minimum number of parts (including units in machines) needed to keep a cell or process flowing smoothly.

## Inventory Turns

A measure of how quickly materials are moving through a facility or through an entire value stream, calculated by dividing some measure of cost of goods by the amount of inventory on hand.

Probably the most common method of calculating inventory turns is to use the annual cost of goods sold (before adding overhead for selling and administrative costs) as the numerator divided by the average inventories on hand during the year. Thus:

$$\text{Inventory turns} = \frac{\text{Annual cost of goods sold}}{\text{Average value of inventories during the year}}$$

Using the cost of goods rather than sales revenues removes one source of variation unrelated to the performance of the production system—fluctuations in selling prices due to market conditions. Using an annual average of inventories rather than an end-of-the-year figure removes another source of variation—an artificial drop in inventories at the end of the year as managers try to show good numbers.

Inventory turns can be calculated for material flows through value streams of any length. However, in making comparisons remember that turns will decline with the length of the value stream, even if performance is equally "lean" all along the value stream. For example, a plant performing only assembly may have turns of 100 or more but when the parts plants supplying the assembly plant are added to the calculation, turns often will fall to 12 or fewer. And if materials are included all the way back to their initial conversion—steel, glass, resins, etc.—turns often will fall to four or fewer. This is because the cost of goods sold at the most downstream step doesn't change but the amount of materials in inventories grows steadily as we add more and more facilities to our calculation.

Inventory turns are a great measure of a lean transformation if the focus is shifted from the absolute number of turns at each facility or in the entire value stream to the rate of increase in turns. Indeed, if turns are calculated accurately using annualized averages of inventories, they can be "the one statistic that can't lie."

*See:* Inventory.

### Inventory Turns Chart for the U.S. Economy

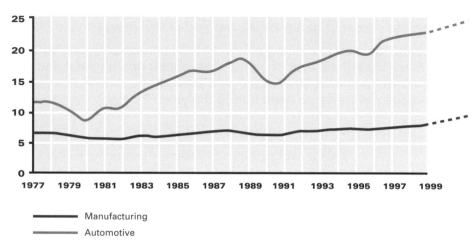

Manufacturing
Automotive

All manufacturing, excluding finished goods at wholesale and retail. Automotive, excluding finished goods at retail.

Note: The U.S. Government does not gather data on cost of goods sold but rather on total sales. Inventory turns therefore have been calculated by dividing total annual sales by average inventories during the year.

## Isolated Islands

A poor arrangement of work flow so people are not in a position to help each other; they are *isolated islands*. The term also can refer to processes outside of a cell or assembly line that run independently to their own rhythm instead of to customer demand. Such islands typically contain a lot of waste, such as excess inventory.

*See*: Cell, Value Stream.

## Jidoka

Providing machines and operators the ability to detect when an abnormal condition has occurred and immediately stop work. This enables operations to build in quality at each process and to separate men and machines for more efficient work. Jidoka is one of the two pillars of the Toyota Production System along with just-in-time.

Jidoka highlights the causes of problems because work stops immediately when a problem first occurs. This leads to improvements in the processes that build in quality by eliminating the root causes of defects.

Jidoka sometimes is called *autonomation*, meaning automation with human intelligence. This is because it gives equipment the ability to distinguish good parts from bad autonomously, without being monitored by an operator. This eliminates the need for operators to continuously watch machines and leads in turn to large productivity gains because one operator can handle several machines, often termed *multiprocess handling*.

The concept of jidoka originated in the early 1900s when Sakichi Toyoda, founder of the Toyota Group, invented a textile loom that stopped automatically when any thread broke. Previously, if a thread broke the loom would churn out mounds of defective fabric, so each machine needed to be watched by an operator. Toyoda's innovation let one operator control many machines. In Japanese, jidoka is a Toyota-created word pronounced exactly the same (and

### The Evolution toward Jidoka

Manual feed and watch machine cycle.

automatic feed

Watch machine cycle.

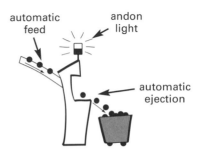

automatic feed

andon light

automatic ejection

Self-monitoring machine.

written in *kanji* almost the same) as the Japanese word for automation, but with the added connotations of humanistic and creating value.

*See:* Andon, Error-Proofing, Fixed-Position Stop System, Inspection, Just-in-Time (JIT), Multiprocess Handling, Toyota Production System (TPS), Visual Management.

## Jishuken

A type of hands-on, learn-by-doing workshop. The term literally means "self-learning" in Japanese.

Jishuken can run in length from one week to several months. Toyota's Operations Management Consulting Division developed this process as a means of developing skills and raising the level of TPS in a certain area, often focusing on supplier operations projects lasting three to four months. Outside of Toyota, jishuken became common in the form of the five-day kaizen workshop. Whatever the length, the goal of any jishuken is to learn by doing and produce an improvement in an area of operations.

*See*: Kaizen Workshop, Toyota Production System (TPS).

## Just-in-Time (JIT) Production

A system of production that makes and delivers just what is needed, just when it is needed, and just in the amount needed. JIT and jidoka are the two pillars of the Toyota Production System. JIT relies on heijunka as a foundation and is comprised of three operating elements: the pull system, takt time, and continuous flow.

JIT aims for the total elimination of all waste to achieve the best possible quality, lowest possible cost and use of resources, and the shortest possible production and delivery lead times. Although simple in principle, JIT demands discipline for effective implementation.

The idea for JIT is credited to Kiichiro Toyoda, the founder of Toyota Motor Corporation, during the 1930s. As manager of the machine shop at Toyota's main plant, Taiichi Ohno said his first steps toward achieving JIT in practice came in 1949–50. (Ohno 1988, p. 31.)

*See:* Continuous Flow, Heijunka, Jidoka, Pull Production, Takt Time, Toyota Production System (TPS).

## Kaikaku
Radical, revolutionary improvement of a value stream to quickly create more value with less waste.

One example would be moving equipment over a weekend so that products formerly fabricated and assembled in batches in isolated process villages are made in single-piece flow in a compact cell. Another example would be quickly switching from stationary to moving assembly for a large product such as a commercial airliner. Also called *breakthrough kaizen*, in comparison with more gradual, *step-by-step kaizen*.

*See:* Kaizen; Plan, Do, Check, Act (PDCA).

## Kaizen
Continuous improvement of an entire value stream or an individual process to create more value with less waste.

There are two levels of kaizen (Rother and Shook 1999, p. 8):

1. System or flow kaizen focusing on the overall value stream. This is kaizen for management.

2. Process kaizen focusing on individual processes. This is kaizen for work teams and team leaders.

### Two Levels of Kaizen

Value-stream mapping is an excellent tool for identifying an entire value stream and determining where flow and process kaizen are appropriate.

*See:* Kaikaku; Plan, Do, Check, Act (PDCA); Process Village; Value-Stream Mapping (VSM).

### Kaizen Promotion Office
*See:* Lean Promotion Office.

### Kaizen Workshop

A group kaizen activity, commonly lasting five days, in which a team identifies and implements a significant improvement in a process.

A common example is creating a continuous flow cell within a week. To do this a kaizen team—including staff experts and consultants as well as operators and line managers—analyzes, implements, tests,

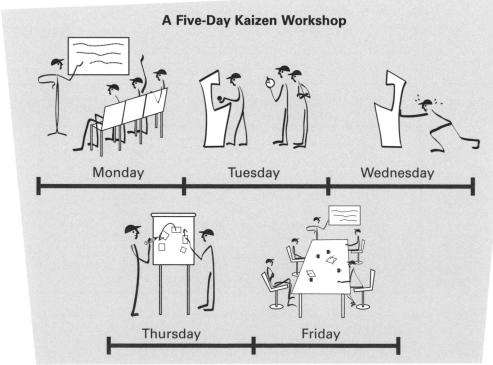

**A Five-Day Kaizen Workshop**

Monday  Tuesday  Wednesday

Thursday  Friday

and standardizes a new cell. Participants first learn continuous flow principles and then go to the gemba to assess actual conditions and plan the cell. Machines then are moved and the new cell is tested. After improvements, the process is standardized and the kaizen team reports out to senior management.

*See:* Gemba; Jishuken; Kaizen; Plan, Do, Check, Act (PDCA).

## Kanban

A kanban is a signaling device that gives authorization and instructions for the production or withdrawal (conveyance) of items in a pull system. The term is Japanese for "sign" or "signboard."

Kanban cards are the best-known and most common example of these signals. They often are slips of card stock, sometimes protected in clear vinyl envelopes, stating information such as part name, part number, external supplier or internal supplying process, pack-out quantity, storage address, and consuming process address. A bar code may be printed on the card for tracking or automatic invoicing.

Besides cards, kanban can be triangular metal plates, colored balls, electronic signals, or any other device that can convey the needed information while preventing the introduction of erroneous instructions.

Whatever the form, kanban have two functions in a production operation: They instruct processes to make products and they instruct material handlers to move products. The former use is called production kanban (or *make kanban*); the latter use is termed withdrawal kanban (or *move kanban*).

**Production kanban** tell an upstream process the type and quantity of products to make for a downstream process. In the simplest situation, a card corresponds to one container of parts, which the upstream process will make for the supermarket ahead of the next downstream process. In large batch situations—for example, a stamping press with very short cycle times and long changeover times—a **signal kanban** is used to trigger production when a minimum quantity of containers is reached. Signal kanban often are triangular in shape and thus often also called *triangle kanban*.

Although a triangle kanban is the standard used in lean manufacturing to schedule a batch production process, it is only one type of signal kanban. Other basic means of controlling batch operations include pattern production and lot making.

**Pattern production** creates a fixed sequence or pattern of production that is continually repeated. However, the actual amount produced each time in the cycle may be unfixed and vary according to customer needs. For example, in an eight-hour cycle, part numbers always are run A through F. (The difficulty of your changeovers may dictate this order.) Inventory in the central market is a function of the length of the pattern-replenishment cycle; a one-day cycle implies one day of inventory must be kept in the market, or a one-week cycle means one week of inventory. The main disadvantage of pattern production is that the sequence is fixed; you can't jump from making part D to part F.

A **lot-making board** involves creating a physical kanban for every container of parts in the system. As material is consumed from the market, the kanban are periodically detached and brought back to the producing process and displayed on a board that highlights all part numbers and displays an outlined shadow space for each of the kanban cards in the system. (Adapted from Smalley 2004, pp. 70–71.)

## Lot-Making Board

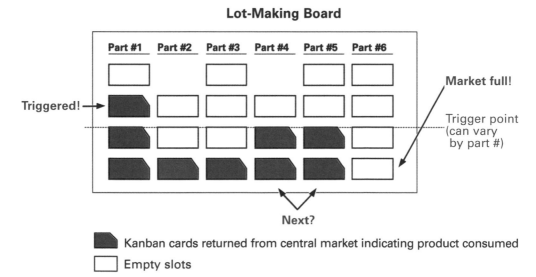

Next?

Kanban cards returned from central market indicating product consumed

Empty slots

A returned kanban card placed on the board in the shadow space indicates inventory has been consumed in the market; unreturned cards represent inventory still in the market. As predefined trigger points are reached, the production operator knows to begin making product to replenish the material in the market.

A lot-making board allows information to come back to the production process more often, signals what has been taken away, and uses smaller increments than the signal kanban. It also provides a visual representation of inventory consumption and highlights emerging problems in the central market. However, it may require many kanban cards, and the cards must be brought back in a timely and reliable manner for the batch board to be accurate. Discipline is required on the part of schedulers and supervisors not to build inventory in advance of when needed.

Withdrawal kanban authorize the conveyance of parts to a downstream process. They often take two forms: **internal** or **interprocess kanban** (for withdrawal from an internal process) and **supplier kanban** (for withdrawal from an external supplier). In their original application around Toyota City, cards commonly were used for both purposes. However, as lean production has spread, supplier kanban for firms at considerable distances have typically taken an electronic form.

Production and withdrawal kanban must work together to create a pull system: At a downstream process, an operator removes a withdrawal kanban when using the first item in a container. This kanban goes in a nearby collection box and is picked up by a material handler. When the material handler returns to the upstream supermarket, the withdrawal kanban is placed on a new container of parts for delivery to the downstream process. As this container is taken from the supermarket, the production kanban on the container is removed and placed in another collection box. The material handler serving the upstream process returns this kanban to that process, where it signals the need to produce one additional container of parts. As long as no parts are produced or moved in the absence of a kanban, a true pull system is maintained.

There are six rules for using kanban effectively:

1. Customer processes order goods in the precise amounts specified on the kanban.

2. Supplier processes produce goods in the precise amounts and sequence specified by the kanban.

3. No items are made or moved without a kanban.

4. All parts and materials always have a kanban attached.

5. Defective parts and incorrect amounts are never sent to the next process.

6. The number of kanban is reduced carefully to lower inventories and reveal problems.

See: Heijunka, Heijunka Box, Just-in-Time (JIT), Pull Production, Supermarket.

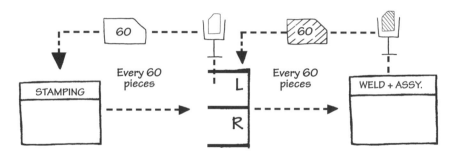

Example of Production and Withdrawal Kanban.

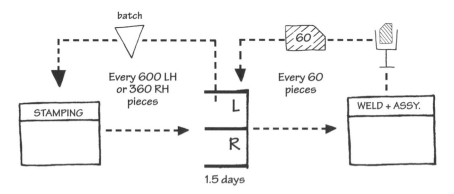

Example of Signal and Withdrawal Kanban.

## Labor Linearity

A philosophy for flexibly manning a production process (in particular a cell) so that the number of operators increases or decreases with production volume. In this way, the amount of human effort required per part produced can be very nearly level (linear) as volume changes. Toyota calls this concept a "flexible manpower line."

*See:* Capital Linearity.

## Lean Consumption

The complementary process to lean production. Lean consumption calls for streamlining all the actions that must be taken to acquire goods and services so that customers receive exactly what they want, when and where they want it, with minimum time and effort.

Companies can streamline consumption by following a six-step thought process, similar to the one for lean manufacturing (Adapted from Womack and Jones 2005, p.15.):

**Principles of Lean Consumption**

1. Solve the customer's problem completely by insuring that all the goods and services work, and work together.

2. Don't waste the customer's time.

3. Provide exactly what the customer wants.

4. Provide what's wanted exactly where it's wanted.

5. Provide what's wanted where it's wanted exactly when it's wanted.

6. Continually aggregate solutions to reduce the customer's time and hassle (bundle a complete range of options from across many organizations).

Applying the concepts requires producers and providers of goods and services to think about consumption not as an isolated decision to buy a specific product, but as a continuing process—a set of activities linking many goods and services over an extended period in order to solve a problem.

For example, when a consumer buys a home computer, his or her objective is not to own a computer but to solve the problem of accessing, processing, storing, and transferring information. The act of buying the computer is not a onetime transaction, but a process of researching, obtaining, integrating, maintaining, upgrading, and, finally, disposing of the computer, and quite possibly, following the same process for software, and peripheral devices.

Lean consumption requires a fundamental shift in the way retailers, service providers, manufacturers, and suppliers think about the relationship between provision and consumption, and the role their customers play in these processes. It also requires collaboration between consumers and providers to minimize total cost and wasted time.

*See*: Consumption and Provision Maps, Lean Production, Lean Provision, Lean Thinking, Value Stream.

## Lean Consumption and Lean Provision Maps

A consumption map is a simple diagram of all the actions customers must take to acquire given goods and services. A provision map is a similar drawing that shows all the actions producers and service companies must perform to deliver these goods and services to customers.

On both the consumption and provision maps, boxes representing individual actions are drawn from left to right in process sequence. Each box is drawn in proportion to the time needed to complete the corresponding action and shaded in proportion to the fraction of value-adding time in each step. Key information, such as total time, value-added time, and first-time quality, also is collected and summarized in a box score for the total consumption and provision process.

To complete the mapping exercise, the two maps are displayed in parallel—one above the other—to show a complete consumption/provision cycle. The combined map helps providers "see" the whole process so they can identify and eliminate wasteful activities in consumption and provision and begin a win-win collaboration by drawing a leaner future-state map. (Womack and Jones 2005, pp. 22-45.)

*See*: Lean Consumption, Lean Provision, Value, Value Stream, Value-Stream Mapping.

# Car Repair Before Lean Processes

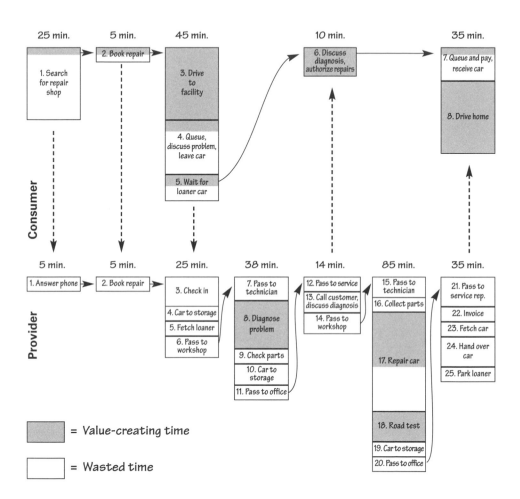

Example of Lean Consumption and Provision Map Before Lean Processes.

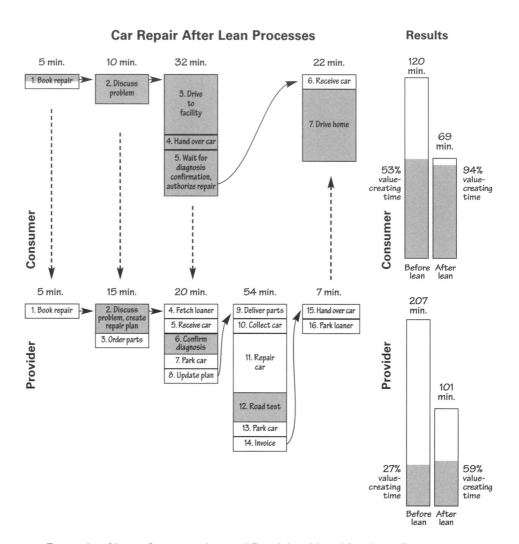

Example of Lean Consumption and Provision Map After Lean Processes.

## Lean Enterprise
A continuing agreement among all the firms sharing the value stream for a product family to correctly specify value from the standpoint of the end customer, remove wasteful actions from the

value stream, and make those actions which do create value occur in continuous flow as pulled by the customer. As soon as this task is completed, the cooperating firms must analyze the results and start the process again through the life of the product family. (Womack and Jones 1996, p. 276.)

A method for performing the needed analysis is described in Womack and Jones 2002.

## Lean Logistics
A pull system with frequent, small-lot replenishment established between each of the firms and facilities along a value stream.

Let's suppose that Firm A (a retailer) sells directly to the end customer and has been replenished by large and infrequent deliveries from Firm B (a manufacturer) based on a sales forecast. The adoption of lean logistics would involve installation of a pull signal from the retailer, as small amounts of goods are sold, to instruct the manufacturer to replenish exactly the amount sold. The manufacturer would in turn instruct its suppliers to replenish quickly the exact amount sent to the retailer, and so on all the way up the value stream.

Lean logistics requires some type of pull signal (EDI, kanban, web-based, etc.), some type of leveling device at each stage of the value stream (heijunka), some type of frequent shipment in small amounts (milk runs linking the retailer with many manufacturers and the manufacturer with many suppliers), and in many cases, various cross-docks for consolidation of loads along the replenishment loops.

*See:* Cross-Dock, Heijunka.

## Lean Production
A business system for organizing and managing product development, operations, suppliers, and customer relations that requires less human effort, less space, less capital, less material, and less time to make products with fewer defects to precise customer desires, compared with the previous system of mass production.

Lean production was pioneered by Toyota after World War II and, as of 1990, typically required half the human effort, half the manufacturing space and capital investment for a given amount of capacity, and a fraction of the development and lead time of mass production systems—while making products in wider variety at lower volumes with many fewer defects. (Womack, Jones, and Roos 1990, p. 13.) The term was coined by John Krafcik, a research assistant at MIT with the International Motor Vehicle Program in the late 1980s.

*See:* Toyota Production System (TPS).
*Compare*: Mass Production.

## Lean Promotion Office

A resource team for a lean transformation, often formed from preexisting industrial engineering, maintenance, facilities management, and quality improvement groups. This team provides value-stream managers technical assistance with:

- Training in lean methods.
- Conducting kaizen workshops.
- Measuring progress.

In addition to the traditional functions, the staff for lean improvement teams often consists of employees freed up in initial transformation efforts who are available to assist with subsequent kaizen activities.

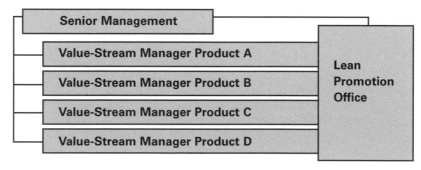

The Lean Promotion Office assists all value-stream managers
and reports to senior management.

## Lean Provision

A term that encompasses *lean manufacturing* (or *lean production*) and all the other steps required to deliver the desired value from producer to customer, often running through a number of organizations.

Most provision value streams, whether for manufactured goods or services like healthcare or travel, are even more complicated than consumption streams. They consume large amounts of provider time and resources and mesh very poorly with consumption streams, creating customer frustration and large amounts of waste. (Womack and Jones 2005, p.8.)

*See*: Lean Consumption and Lean Provision Maps, Lean Consumption, Lean Production, Lean Thinking, Value Stream.

## Lean Thinking

A five-step thought process proposed by Womack and Jones in 1996 to guide managers through a lean transformation. The five principles are:

1. Specify value from the standpoint of the end customer by product family.

2. Identify all the steps in the value stream for each product family, eliminating whenever possible those steps that do not create value.

3. Make the value-creating steps occur in tight sequence so the product will flow smoothly toward the customer.

4. As flow is introduced, let customers pull value from the next upstream activity.

5. As value is specified, value streams are identified, wasted steps are removed, and flow and pull are introduced, begin the process again and continue it until a state of perfection is reached in which perfect value is created with no waste.

(Adapted from Womack and Jones 1996, p.10.)

*See:* Toyota Production System (TPS).

## Level Production

*See:* Heijunka.

## Level Selling

A stance toward customers that presumes the level of demand for many products is relatively stable but often is perturbed by production and sales systems.

For example: Monthly and quarterly sales bonuses for sales staffs tend to bunch orders at the end of the reporting period. Promotional activities, such as service specials at car dealers, tend to create spikes and troughs in demand for service parts unrelated to actual customer desires. And producing large batches of goods far in advance based on forecasts almost certainly leads to surpluses of some goods, which then must be sold using special promotions that temporarily "create" demand.

Level selling involves the elimination of artificial sales spikes—what Toyota calls "created demand"—by changing sales incentives, eliminating promotions, producing in small batches to replenish what customers have just purchased, and forming long-term relations with customers so that future demand can be better anticipated and smoothed. Any variations in demand remaining after production and sales system distortions have been removed are real variations. A truly lean production and selling system must be capable of responding to them.

*See:* Build-to-Order, Demand Amplification, Heijunka.

## Machine Cycle Time
*See:* Cycle Time.

## Mass Production

A business system developed early in the 20th century to organize and manage product development, production operations, purchasing, and customer relations. Typically:

• The design process is sequential rather than simultaneous.

• The production process has a rigid hierarchy with jobs divided into thinking/planning and doing.

• The product is taken to the process rather than the reverse.

• Suppliers *work-to-print* after selection through bids for piece prices rather than total cost to the customer.

• Materials are delivered infrequently in large batches.

• Information is managed through high-level systems instructing each production step what to do next and pushing products downstream.

• Customers often are subject to push selling to meet quotas and clear inventories produced to erroneous forecasts.

*See:* Batch-and-Queue.
*Compare:* Lean Production.

## Material Flow
The movement of physical items through the entire value stream.

In *mass production*, products travel to centralized processes in large batches, pushed forward on the instructions of a master scheduling system. In *lean production*, the process steps for different product families are moved together, whenever possible, into tight process sequence so small amounts of product can flow directly from step to step at the pull of the next downstream process and of the end customer.

*See:* Information Flow, Just-in-Time (JIT), Lean Production, Mass Production.

### Current-State Material Flow in Mass Production

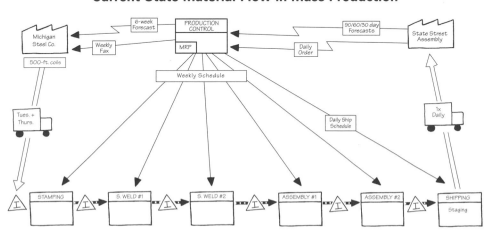

Material flow is shown in blue. Map symbols on
material flow are explained in Appendix A.

## Material Handling
Moving necessary materials through a production process within a facility.

In a lean production system material handling does much more than just deliver materials. A lean material-handling system can serve as the primary means of carrying production instructions. A well-designed system also can improve the efficiency of production operators by taking away wasteful activities such a getting materials, wrestling with dunnage, and reaching for parts.

### Fixed-time, unfixed-quantity conveyance
In this type of handling system, a material handler performs a standard route through a facility at precisely determined time intervals such as every 20 minutes. The amount of material moved each time may vary, but the time interval is exact. During this interval the material handler follows a predetermined, standard route, picking up kanban cards signaling what materials to deliver next, and delivering the materials to production locations. This system often is coupled with a heijunka box in which the withdrawal intervals in the columns of the box correspond to the time required for the standard material handling route. This type of system often is employed in assembly operations where a large number of components need to be delivered to many points along a line. It also is called *mizusumashi* or *waterspider conveyance*.

### Fixed-quantity, unfixed-time conveyance
This type of handling system acts on signals from downstream locations to deliver exactly the materials needed when they are needed and in the right amounts. The material handler is signaled to collect materials from a preceding process when a trigger point or predetermined stock level is reached. Because the material handler collects a standard quantity of materials from the upstream process (such as one tray or one pallet or one skid), the quantity of material is fixed but the timing of conveyance varies with need. This type of system often is employed in facilities with storage areas for materials that are produced in batches due to long changeover times. As the cell or machine depletes the materials in the storage area, a signal is triggered for the material handler to replenish from upstream processes the amounts consumed. This type of system often is termed a *call system* or a *call-parts system*.

It is less common but possible to use waterspider conveyance in conjunction with fixed-quantity, unfixed-time conveyance. In this arrangement, the material handler will dart around from one production process to another picking up fixed quantities of materials from varying processes on a route that changes with time.

*See:* Heijunka Box, Paced Withdrawal.

## Milk Run

A method to speed the flow of materials between facilities by routing vehicles to make multiple pick-ups and drop-offs at many facilities. By making frequent pick-ups and drop-offs with milk-run vehicles connecting a number of facilities rather than waiting to accumulate a truckload for direct shipment between two facilities, it is possible to reduce inventories and response times along a value stream. Milk runs between facilities are similar in concept to material handling routes within facilities.

*See:* Lean Logistics, Material Handling.

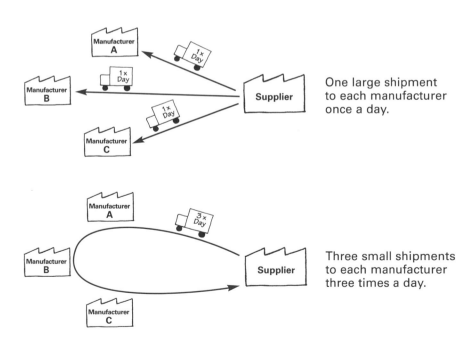

One large shipment to each manufacturer once a day.

Three small shipments to each manufacturer three times a day.

**Mistake-Proofing**
*See:* Error-Proofing.


**Monument**
Any design, scheduling, or production technology with large-scale requirements and lengthy changeover times that requires designs, orders, or products to be brought to the technology and to wait in a queue for processing.

*See:* Capital Linearity, Right-Sized Tools.


**Muda, Mura, Muri**
Three terms often used together in the Toyota Production System (and called the Three Ms) that collectively describe wasteful practices to be eliminated.

**Muda**
Any activity that consumes resources without creating value for the customer. Within this general category it is useful to distinguish between *type one muda*, consisting of activities that cannot be eliminated immediately, and *type two muda*, consisting of activities that can be eliminated quickly through kaizen.

An example of type one muda is a rework operation after a paintbooth, which is required to obtain a finish acceptable to the customer from a paint process that is not highly capable. Because a completely capable paint process for fine finishes has eluded manufacturers for decades, it is not likely that this type of muda can be eliminated quickly.

An example of type two muda is multiple movements of products and inventories between steps in a fabrication and assembly process. These steps can be quickly eliminated in a kaizen workshop by moving production equipment and operators into a smoothly flowing cell.

**Mura**
Unevenness in an operation; for example, a gyrating schedule not caused by end-consumer demand but rather by the production system, or an uneven work pace in an operation causing operators to hurry and then wait. Unevenness often can be eliminated by managers through level scheduling and careful attention to the pace of work.

## Muri

Overburdening equipment or operators by requiring them to run at a higher or harder pace with more force and effort for a longer period of time than equipment designs and appropriate workforce management allow.

## Muda, Mura, and Muri in Conjunction

A simple illustration shows how muda, mura, and muri often are related so that eliminating one also eliminates the others.

Suppose that a firm needs to transport six tons of material to its customer and is considering its options. One is to pile all six tons on one truck and make a single trip. But this would be muri because it would overburden the truck (rated for only three tons) leading to breakdowns, which also would lead to muda and mura.

**Muri = overburdened**

**Mura = unevenness, fluctuation, variation**

**Muda = waste**

**No Muri, Mura, or Muda**

A second option is to make two trips, one with four tons and the other with two. But this would be mura because the unevenness of materials arriving at the customer would create jam-ups on the receiving dock followed by too little work. This option also would create muri, because on one trip the truck still is overburdened, and muda as well, because the uneven pace of work would cause the waste of waiting by the customer's receiving employees.

A third option is to load two tons on the truck and make three trips. But this would be muda, even if not mura and muri, because the truck would be only partially loaded on each trip.

The only way to eliminate muda, mura, and muri is to load the truck with three tons (its rated capacity) and make two trips.

*See:* Heijunka.

### Multimachine Handling
The work practice of assigning operators to operate more than one machine in a process village layout. Requires the separation of human work from machine work, and usually is facilitated by applying jidoka and auto-eject to the machines.

*See:* Jidoka, Multiprocess Handling.

Single Machine Handling.

Multimachine Handling.

## Multiprocess Handling

The work practice of assigning operators to operate more than one process in a product-flow oriented layout. Requires training operators to operate different types of machines (e.g., bender, crimper, and tester) so they can walk products through cellularized operations. (Also known as *cross-training*.)

This practice contrasts with the typical mass production practice of placing operators in separate departments—turning, milling, grinding —where they work only one type of machine and make batches of parts to transfer to other processes in other departments.

*See:* Multimachine Handling.

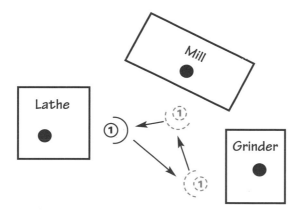

Operator working different types of machines in a cell.

## Nemawashi

The process of gaining acceptance and preapproval for a proposal by evaluating first the idea and then the plan with management and stakeholders to get input, anticipate resistance, and align the proposed change with other perspectives and priorities in the organization. Formal approval comes in a meeting to sign off on the final version of the proposal. The term literally means "preparing the ground for planting" in Japanese.

*See*: Policy Deployment.

## Nonvalue-Creating Time
*See:* Cycle Time.

## Obeya
Obeya in Japanese means simply "big room." At Toyota it has become a major project-management tool, used especially in product development, to enhance effective and timely communication. Similar in concept to traditional "war rooms," an obeya will contain highly visual charts and graphs depicting program timing, milestones and progress to date, and countermeasures to existing timing or technical problems. Project leaders will have desks in the obeya as will others at appropriate points in the program timing. The purpose is to ensure project success and shorten the PDCA cycle.

*See:* Plan, Do, Check, Act (PDCA).

## Ohno, Taiichi (1912–1990)
The Toyota executive widely credited as the chief architect of the Toyota Production System (TPS). Author of several important books about TPS.

## One-Piece Flow
Making and moving one piece at a time.

*See:* Continuous Flow, Every Product Every Interval (EPEx), Single Minute Exchange of Die (SMED).

## Operation
Work that is done on an item by a machine or person.

*See:* Process.

## Operational Availability versus Operating Rate

**Operational availability** is the fraction of time a machine functions properly when needed. (Also called *operable rate*.) The **operating rate** is the amount of time in a time period (shift, day, etc.) that a machine is used to make something.

Use of an automobile illustrates the difference between the two terms. The operational availability is the percentage of time the car runs properly when needed. The operating rate is the percentage of time per day the car is actually driven.

Lean Thinkers use the distinction to illustrate a trap in traditional thinking about efficiency. From a lean perspective, a high operating rate is not necessarily desirable. Whether an operating rate is good or bad depends on whether or not the equipment is producing just what is needed (good) or overproducing (bad). On the other hand, the ideal operational availability is 100% because it refers to how well a machine runs when needed.

*See:* Overall Equipment Effectiveness.

## Operator Balance Chart (OBC)

A graphic tool that assists the creation of continuous flow in a multistep, multioperator process by distributing operator work elements in relation to takt time. (Also called an *operator loading diagram* or a *yamazumi board*.)

An OBC (shown on the next page) uses vertical bars to represent the total amount of work each operator must do compared to takt time. The vertical bar for each operator is built by stacking small bars representing individual work elements, with the height of each element proportional to the amount of time required. Creating an operator balance chart helps with the critical task of redistributing work elements among operators. This is essential for minimizing the number of operators needed by making the amount of work for each operator very nearly equal to, but slightly less than, takt time.

*See:* Yamazumi Board.

**Operator Balance Chart (OBC)**

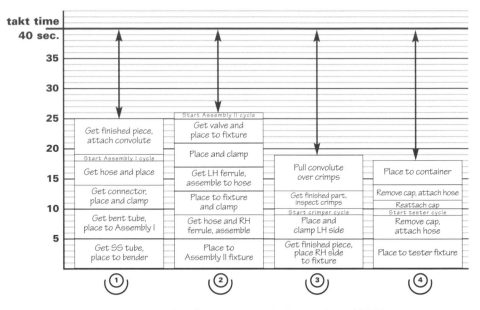

takt time
40 sec.

35

30

25

20

15

10

5

|  |  |  |  |
|---|---|---|---|
| Get finished piece, attach convolute | Get valve and place to fixture | | |
| | Start Assembly II cycle | | |
| Start Assembly I cycle | Place and clamp | Pull convolute over crimps | Place to container |
| Get hose and place | Get LH ferrule, assemble to hose | | Remove cap, attach hose |
| Get connector, place and clamp | Place to fixture and clamp | Get finished part, inspect crimps | Reattach cap |
| | | Start crimper cycle | Start tester cycle |
| Get bent tube, place to Assembly I | Get hose and RH ferrule, assemble | Place and clamp LH side | Remove cap, attach hose |
| Get SS tube, place to bender | Place to Assembly II fixture | Get finished piece, place RH side to fixture | Place to tester fixture |

① ② ③ ④

An example of an operator balance chart (OBC).

## Operator Cycle Time
*See:* Cycle Time.

## Out-of-Cycle Work
Tasks of operators in multioperator processes which require the operator to break the pace of work or leave the area.

Examples include retrieving parts from storage locations and moving finished items to downstream processes. These tasks should be removed from the operator's *standardized work* and given to support staff such as material handlers and team leaders, who work outside of takt-time-based continuous flow.

*See:* Standardized Work.

## Overall Equipment Effectiveness (OEE)
A total productive maintenance (TPM) measure of how effectively equipment is being used.

OEE is calculated from three elements: The **availability rate** measures downtime losses from equipment failures and adjustments as a percentage of scheduled time. The **performance rate** measures operating speed losses—running at speeds lower than design speed and stoppages lasting a few seconds. The **quality rate** expresses losses due to scrap and rework as a percentage of total parts run.

These elements are multiplied to obtain OEE:

Availability Rate x Performance Rate x Quality Rate = OEE

If Availability is 90%, Performance is 95%, and Quality is 99% then

0.90 x 0.95 x 0.99 = 84.6% OEE

OEE typically focuses on what are termed the *six major losses*— failures, adjustments, minor stoppages, reduced operating speeds, scrap, and rework—but some companies add other measures judged important to their business.

*See:* Total Productive Maintenance (TPM).

## Overproduction

Producing more, sooner or faster than is required by the next process. Ohno considered overproduction to be the most grievous form of waste because it generates and hides other wastes, such as inventories, defects, and excess transport.

*See:* Batch-and-Queue, Ohno, Seven Wastes.

## Paced Withdrawal

The practice of releasing production instructions to work areas and withdrawing completed product from work areas at a fixed, frequent pace. This practice can be used as a means of linking material flows with information flow.

In the illustration below, the material handler circulates through the entire route every 20 minutes. The handler begins by withdrawing production instructions (production kanban) from a heijunka box, then delivers the kanban to a production process where they are the signal to produce goods.

The handler picks up finished products from the production process and takes these to the supermarket. There the handler picks up production kanban from the collection box, takes these to the heijunka box for insertion in the box, and withdraws the next increment of production kanban from the appropriate column in the box as the cycle starts again.

Paced withdrawal serves to prevent overproduction and quickly alerts managers—in this case, in less than 20 minutes—if there is a production problem.

*See:* Every Product Every Interval (EPEx), Heijunka Box, Milk Run, Pull Production.

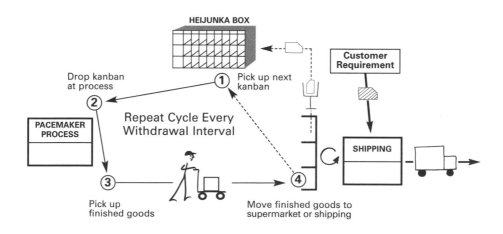

Typical paced withdrawal in a plant environment.

## Pacemaker Process

Any process along a value stream that sets the pace for the entire stream. (The pacemaker process should not be confused with a bottleneck process, which necessarily constrains downstream processes due to a lack of capacity.)

The pacemaker process usually is near the customer end of the value stream, often the final assembly cell. However, if products flow from an upstream process to the end of the stream in a FIFO sequence, the pacemaker may be at this upstream process.

*See:* FIFO.

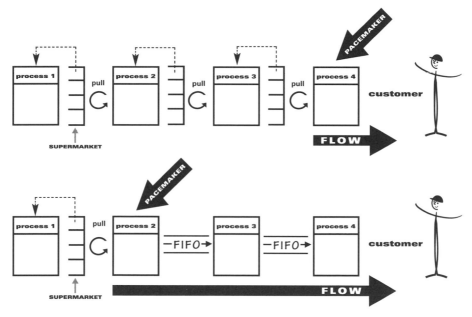

Selecting the pacemaker process.

## Pack-Out Quantity

The number of items a customer (whether internal in a facility or external) wants packed in a container for conveyance and shipping. Note that a pallet or skid of the product may consist of a number of containers.

*See:* Pitch.

## Perfection
When a process provides pure value, as defined by the customer, with no waste of any sort.

*See:* Plan, Do, Check, Act (PDCA).

## Pitch
The amount of time needed in a production area to make one container of products.

The formula for pitch is:

takt time x pack-out quantity = pitch

For example, if takt time (available production time per day divided by customer demand per day) is one minute and the pack-out quantity is 20, then: 1 minute x 20 pieces = pitch of 20 minutes

Pitch, in conjunction with the use of a heijunka box and material handling based on paced withdrawal, helps set the takt image and pace of a facility or process.

Note that the term pitch also is sometimes used to indicate the span or time of a person's job.

*See:* Heijunka Box, Paced Withdrawal, Pack-Out Quantity, Takt Time.

## Plan, Do, Check, Act (PDCA)
An improvement cycle based on the scientific method of proposing a change in a process, implementing the change, measuring the results, and taking appropriate action. It also is known as the *Deming Cycle* or *Deming Wheel* after W. Edwards Deming, who introduced the concept in Japan in the 1950s.

The PDCA cycle has four stages:

**Plan:** Determine goals for a process and needed changes to achieve them.

**Do:** Implement the changes.

**Check:** Evaluate the results in terms of performance.

**Act:** Standardize and stabilize the change or begin the cycle again, depending on the results.

A common version of the PDCA wheel is shown below:

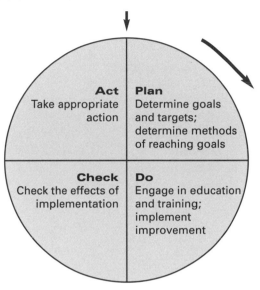

| **Act** Take appropriate action | **Plan** Determine goals and targets; determine methods of reaching goals |
| **Check** Check the effects of implementation | **Do** Engage in education and training; implement improvement |

Toyota frequently employs PDCA, but changes the terminology slightly:

**Grasp the Situation or "Go See"**

| **Standardize** Stabilize effective actions | **Plan** Determine goals, deliverables, responsibilities, and metrics |
| **Reflect** Check the effects of implementation | **Try** Implement improvement |

## Plan For Every Part (PFEP)

A detailed plan for each part used in a production process, showing everything relevant to managing the process with no errors or waste. This is a critical tool in the Toyota Production System.

A plan will include the part number, its dimensions, the amount used daily, the precise location of use, the precise location of storage, order frequency, the supplier, pack-out quantity, transit time from the supplier, container size and weight, and any other relevant information. The point is to precisely specify every aspect of the handling and use of every part. (Harris, Harris, and Wilson 2003, pp. 15–22.)

*See:* Material Handling, Pack-Out Quantity.

## Plan For Every Person

A training and development schedule for employees, showing the skills needed and the skills attained.

In the sample plan below, the needed skills are arrayed across the top with employees listed in the left column. The shading is in proportion to the level of skills attained. The dates in empty or

| Skills Training Matrix | | □ Unable to do operation (LOSS)  ▨ Can generally do operation (TIE)  ▤ Can do operation well (WIN) | | | | Factory name: By: | | | Foreman: Date: | | |
|---|---|---|---|---|---|---|---|---|---|---|---|

| No. | Operator Name | Priming | Mounting | Reflow | Cleaning | Visual inspect. | Corrections | Soldering | Powder Coating | Curing | Sealing | External view inspection | Tie bar card | Electrical char. | Packaging | Current Date | Target Date |
|---|---|---|---|---|---|---|---|---|---|---|---|---|---|---|---|---|---|
| 1 | Worker A | ▤ | ▤ | ▤ | ▤ | ▤ | ◹ | ◹ | 12/30 | 12/30 | 12/30 | 12/30 | | | | | |
| | | | | | | | 11/30 | 11/30 | | | | | | | | | |
| 2 | Worker B | 12/30 | 12/30 | 11/30 | ◹ | | | | | | | | | | | | |
| 3 | Worker C | | | | | | ◹ | ◹ | ◹ | ▤ | ▤ | ▤ | | | | | |
| | | | | | | | 11/30 | 11/30 | 12/30 | | | | | | | | |
| 4 | Worker D | | | | | | ◹ 11/30 | ▤ | ▤ | ▤ | ▤ | ▤ | ▤ | ▤ | ◹ 11/30 | | |
| | | | | | | | | | | | | | | | | | |
| | | | | | | | | | | | | | | | | | |

partially shaded boxes are targets for attaining the needed skills. This tool is particularly useful for assessing progress in training employees in the multiple skills needed for multiprocess handling.

*See:* Multiprocess Handling.

## Point-of-Use Storage
Storing production parts and materials as close as possible to the operations that require them.

## Poka-Yoke
*See:* Error-Proofing.

## Policy Deployment
A management process that aligns—both vertically and horizontally— a firm's functions and activities with its strategic objectives. A specific plan—typically annual—is developed with precise goals, actions, timelines, responsibilities, and measures.

In the example policy deployment matrix (shown on the next page), a firm is converting current batch-and-queue manufacturing operations to continuous flow. To do this it selects a number of projects to: (1) Introduce value-stream managers; (2) create a lean promotion office with the necessary skills; and (3) launch specific activities to convert batch-and-queue operations to continuous flow. Even as the firm does this it deselects many other projects proposed by different parts of the organization. Project targets, flowing from project selection, set improvement goals and timetables.

Policy deployment, also known by the Japanese term *hoshin kanri*, may start as a top-down process when a firm launches a lean conversion. However, once the major goals are set, it should become a top-down and bottom-up process involving a dialogue between senior managers and project teams about the resources and time both available and needed to achieve the targets. This dialogue often is called *catchball* (or nemawashi) as ideas are tossed back and forth like a ball.

## Policy Deployment Matrix

| Identify value stream by product | Introduce continuous flow and pull | Dramatically improve quality | Objectives / Selected Projects / Improvement Targets / Target Dollar Results (current year) | Perform six major improvement activities per month | Introduce value-stream managers within six months | Form lean enterprises within one year | Product line reorganization | Improvement function team | Product family A team | Product family B team | Product family C team | Product family D team |
|---|---|---|---|---|---|---|---|---|---|---|---|---|
| X | | | Reorganize by product families | | | X | X | | | | | |
| | X | | Create productivity and quality improvement function | X | | | | X | | | | |
| X | X | X | Create lean enterprises with suppliers | | X | | | | X | X | X | X |
| | | | **Selected Projects** — **Objectives** / **Improvement Targets** — **Target Dollar Results (current year)** | | | | | Improvement Teams | | | | |
| | X | | Reduce inventory by $30M | X | | | | | | | | |
| | | X | Reduce cost of quality by $15M | X | | | | | | | | |
| | X | | Reduce labor costs by $30M | X | | | | | | | | |

Source: Womack and Jones 1996, p. 96.

The objective is to match available resources with desirable projects so that only projects that are desirable, important, and achievable are authorized. (This is to avoid the practice in many organizations of embarking on many improvement initiatives that are popular in parts of the organization but failing to complete them for lack of cross-function agreement and resources.)

As a firm progresses with its lean transformation and gains experience with policy deployment, the process should become much more bottom-top-bottom, with each part of the organization proposing actions to senior management to improve performance. A mature lean organization, such as Toyota, may call this process *policy management* rather than policy deployment.

*See:* Plan, Do, Check, Act (PDCA).

## Preventive Maintenance

An equipment servicing approach considered a precursor to Total Productive Maintenance that is based on regularly scheduled checking and overhauling by maintenance personnel to decrease breakdowns and increase equipment life.

In lean manufacturing, hourly workers have daily responsibilities for performing basic preventive maintenance tasks like checking lubrication levels, the condition of filters, and the tightness of nuts and bolts.

*Compare*: Total Productive Maintenance.

## Process

A series of individual operations that must occur in a specific sequence to create a design, complete an order, or produce a product.

## Process Capacity Sheet

*See:* Standardized Work.

## Process Village

A grouping of activities by type rather than in the sequence needed to design or make a product.

Historically, most organizations created process villages for activities ranging from grinding on the shop floor to credit checking in the office. Lean organizations try to relocate process steps, wherever possible, from villages into process sequences for product families.

The illustration on the following page shows two plant layouts contrasting process village and process sequence material flow in a bicycle plant.

*See:* Mass Production, Material Flow.

## Process Village Layout vs. Process Sequence Layout

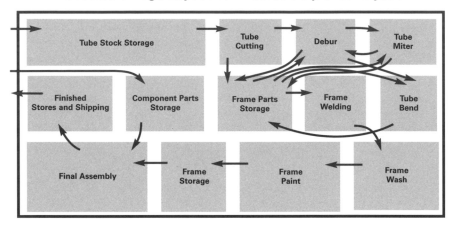

Process village layout.

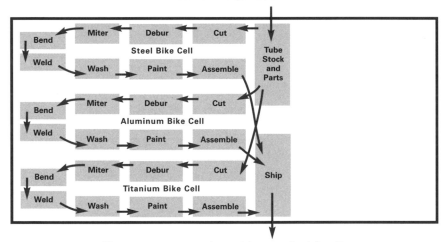

Process sequence layout by product family.

## Processing Time
*See:* Cycle Time.

## Product Family

A product and its variants passing through similar processing steps and common equipment just prior to shipment to the customer. The significance of product families for Lean Thinkers is that they are the unit of analysis for value-stream maps, which are defined from the most downstream step just before the customer.

Note that product families can be defined from the standpoint of any customer along an extended value stream, ranging from the ultimate customer (the end consumer) to intermediate customers within the production process.

For example: In a power tools business, a product family might be defined as medium-sized electric drills utilizing a common chassis and passing through a common assembly cell as the last manufacturing step before shipment directly to end consumers.

Alternatively, the product family might be defined as the drive motor and its variants assembled in a common cell just prior to shipment to the drill manufacturer customer.

Or a product family might be defined as the drive motor stator and its variants going through a common manufacturing process just prior to shipment to the drive motor customer.

*See:* Product Family Matrix, Value-Stream Mapping (VSM).


## Product Family Matrix

A chart constructed by Lean Thinkers to identify appropriate product families.

In the illustration on the next page, a firm with seven product lines, as perceived by its customers, arrayed its assembly steps and equipment across the top of a product family matrix and quickly found a common path for Products A, B, and C, which it then value stream mapped as a product family.

*See:* Product Family, Value-Stream Mapping (VSM).

## Product Family Matrix

| | | Assembly Steps and Equipment | | | | | | | |
|---|---|:-:|:-:|:-:|:-:|:-:|:-:|:-:|:-:|
| | | 1 | 2 | 3 | 4 | 5 | 6 | 7 | 8 |
| **PRODUCTS** | A | X | X | X | | X | X | | |
| | B | X | X | X | X | X | X | | |
| | C | X | X | X | | X | X | X | |
| | D | | X | X | X | | | X | X |
| | E | | X | X | X | | | X | X |
| | F | X | | X | | X | X | X | |
| | G | X | | X | | X | X | X | |

Source: Rother and Shook 1999, p. 6.

## Production Analysis Board

A display—often a large whiteboard—located beside a process to show actual performance compared with planned performance.

The board in the illustration (on the next page) shows the performance of a process on an hourly basis with planned versus actual production. When production does not correspond to the plan, the problem is recorded and a cause is sought.

Note that a process regulated by pull signals rather than a preset schedule will record the amounts requested by the next downstream process, which may vary from plan during a shift or day, and compare the requested amounts with actual production.

A production analysis board can be an important visual management tool, particularly as a firm begins its transformation to lean production. However, it is important to understand that the appropriate use for the production analysis board is as a problem-identification and problem-solving tool and not, as often is misunderstood, as a tool for scheduling production. The tool also is sometimes called a *production control board*, a *progress control board*, or—more appropriately—a *problem-solving board*.

*See:* Plan, Do, Check, Act (PDCA).

## Production Analysis Board

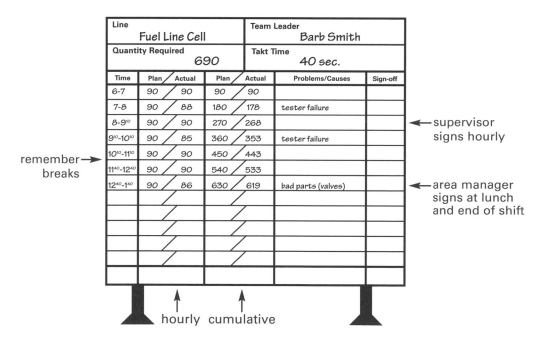

Source: Rother and Harris 2001, p. 86.

## Production Control

The task of controlling and pacing production so that products flow smoothly and quickly to meet customer requirements.

At Toyota, the production control department evolved as the key corporate function to speed the pace of production when behind and to restrain it when ahead. This contrasts with typical mass production firms where production control is responsible for isolated tasks, such as material requirements planning and logistics.

## Production Lead Time

*See:* Cycle Time.

## Production Preparation Process (3P)

A disciplined method for designing a lean production process for a new product or for fundamentally redesigning the production process for an existing product when the design or customer demand change substantially.

A cross-functional 3P team examines the total production process, developing a number of alternatives for each process step and evaluating these against lean criteria. Using simple materials, the team then mocks up the process to test assumptions before equipment is ordered or installed in the final configuration.

*Compare*: Kaizen, Kaizen Workshops.

## Production Smoothing

*See:* Heijunka.

## Pull Production

A method of production control in which downstream activities signal their needs to upstream activities. Pull production strives to eliminate overproduction and is one of the three major components of a complete just-in-time production system.

In pull production, a downstream operation, whether within the same facility or in a separate facility, provides information to the upstream operation, often via a kanban card, about what part or material is needed, the quantity needed, and when and where it is needed. Nothing is produced by the upstream supplier process until the downstream customer process signals a need. This is the opposite of push production.

There are three basic types of pull production systems:

### Supermarket Pull System

The most basic and widespread type, also known as a *fill-up* or *replenishment* or *a-type pull system*. In a supermarket pull system each process has a store—a supermarket—that holds an amount of each product it produces. Each process simply produces to replenish what is withdrawn from its supermarket. Typically, as material is withdrawn from the supermarket by the downstream customer process, a kanban or other type of information will be sent upstream to the supplying process to withdraw product. This will authorize the upstream process to replace what was withdrawn.

Each process is responsible for the replenishment of its supermarket, so daily management of the worksite is relatively simple and kaizen opportunities are relatively easy to see. The disadvantage of a supermarket system is that a process must carry an inventory of all part numbers it produces, which may not be feasible if the number of part numbers is large.

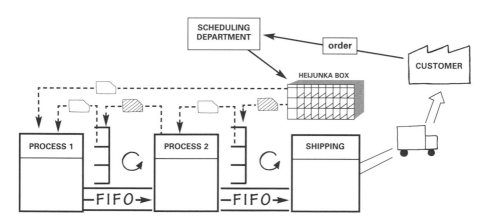

Mixed Supermarket and Sequential Pull System.

### Sequential Pull System

A sequential pull system—also known as a *b-type pull system*—may be used when there are too many part numbers to hold inventory of each in a supermarket. Products are essentially "made-to-order" while overall system inventory is minimized.

In a sequential system, the scheduling department must set the right mix and quantity of products to be produced. This can be done by placing production kanban cards in a heijunka box, often at the beginning of each shift. These production instructions then are sent to the process at the upstream end of the value stream. Often this is done in the form of a "sequence list," sometimes called a "sequential tablet." Each following process simply produces in sequence the items delivered to it by the preceding upstream process. FIFO of individual products must be maintained throughout.

A sequential system creates pressure to maintain short and predictable lead times. In order for this system to work effectively, the pattern of customer orders must be well understood. If orders are hard to predict, production lead time must either be very short (less than order lead time) or an adequate store of finished goods must be held.

A sequential system requires strong management to maintain, and improving it may be a challenge on the shop floor.

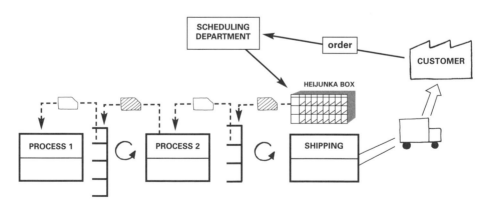

Supermarket Pull System.

## Mixed Supermarket and Sequential Pull System

Supermarket and sequential pull systems may be used together in a *mixed system*—also known as a *c-type pull system*. A mixed system may be appropriate when an 80/20 rule applies, with a small percentage of part numbers (perhaps 20%) accounting for the majority (perhaps 80%) of daily production volume. Often an analysis is performed to segment part numbers by volume into (A) high, (B) medium, (C) low, and (D) infrequent orders. Type D may represent special order or service parts. To handle these low-running items, a special type D kanban may be created to represent not a specific part number but rather an amount of capacity. The sequence of production for the type D products is then determined by the method the scheduling department uses for sequential pull system part numbers.

Such a mixed system enables both supermarket and sequential systems to be applied selectively and the benefits of each are obtained, even in environments where the demand is complex and varied. The two systems may run together, side-by-side horizontally, throughout an entire value stream, or may be used for a given part number at different locations along its individual value stream.

A mixed system may make it more difficult to balance work and to identify abnormal conditions. It also can be more difficult to manage and conduct kaizen. Therefore, discipline is required to make a mixed system work effectively. (Adapted from Smalley 2004, pp. 17–20.)

*See:* Just-in-Time (JIT), Overproduction.
*Compare:* Push Production.

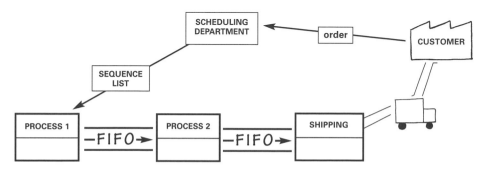

Sequential Pull System.

## Push Production

Processing large batches of items at a maximum rate, based on forecasted demand, then moving them to the next downstream process or into storage, regardless of the actual pace of work in the next process. Such a system makes it virtually impossible to establish the smooth flow of work from one process to the next that is the hallmark of lean production.

*See:* Batch-and-Queue, Production Control.
*Compare:* Pull Production.

## Quality Assurance

*See:* Inspection.

## Quality Control Circle

A small group of workers and their team leader who collectively identify problems in their work area, analyze them, and provide solutions.

In contrast to other companies, particularly in the West, circles at Toyota are integrated into the overall total quality control system and shop-floor organization. Toyota circles meet two to three times per month from 30 to 60 minutes.

Management expert Peter Drucker noted that circles were used widely in the U.S. during World War II. They reached their greatest success in Japan after the war. The U.S. re-imported them during the quality movement of the 1970s and 1980s. Unfortunately, circles at U.S. companies often were not integrated into an overall continuous improvement effort. These isolated circles dissolved as the fad faded in the late 1980s.

*See*: Team Leader, Total Quality Control.

## Quality Function Deployment (QFD)

A visual decision-making procedure for cross-functional product project teams that develops a common understanding of customer needs (the "voice of the customer") and a consensus on the final engineering specifications of the product to meet those needs that has the commitment of the entire team.

QFD integrates the perspectives of team members from different disciplines, ensures that their efforts are focused on resolving key trade-offs in a consistent manner against measurable performance targets for the product, and deploys these decisions through successive levels of detail. The use of QFD eliminates expensive backflows and rework as projects near launch.

A hallmark of QFD is the "house of quality" diagram that visually identifies spoken and unspoken needs of customers, translates them into actions and designs, and communicates them throughout the organization. It also allows customers to prioritize their requirements. Suppliers providing critical components are often involved in QFD sessions at the start of the design process.

*See*: Value.

## Red Tagging

Labeling unneeded items for removal from a production or office area during a Five S exercise.

Red tags are attached to unneeded tools, equipment, and supplies. Tagged items are placed in a holding area where they are evaluated for other uses within a facility or company. Those with no alternative uses are discarded. Red tagging helps achieve the first *S* of the Five S exercise, which calls for separating needed from unneeded items.

*See:* Five Ss.

## Resident Engineer

A component engineer from a supplier who is sent to Toyota to work jointly with its engineers on development projects or to solve problems; sometimes called a "guest engineer."

*See:* Design-In.

## Right-Sized Tools

Process equipment that is highly capable, easy to maintain (and therefore available to produce whenever needed), quick to changeover, easy to move, and designed to be installed in small increments of capacity to facilitate capital and labor linearity.

Examples of right-sized tools are small washing machines, heat treatment ovens, and paint booths that can be placed in process sequence in cells to facilitate continuous flow.

*See:* Capital Linearity, Labor Linearity.
*Compare:* Monuments.

## Safety Stock

*See:* Inventory.

## Sensei

The Japanese term for "teacher." Used by Lean Thinkers to denote a master of lean knowledge as a result of years of experience in transforming the gemba (the place where work actually is done). The sensei also must be an easily understood and inspiring teacher.

*Compare:* Change Agent.

## Sequential Pull

*See*: Pull Production.

## Set-Based Concurrent Engineering

The process of developing and prototyping many alternative designs at the outset of a product development program, and delaying the selection of the final design until the performance of the alternatives can be compared.

This process, as practiced by Toyota and Denso in particular, yields substantial organizational learning. It takes less time and costs less in the long term than typical point-based engineering systems that select a design solution early in the development process, with the typical consequence of false starts, rework, failed projects, and minimal learning.

## Setup Reduction

The process of reducing the amount of time needed to changeover a process from the last part for the previous product to the first good part for the next product.

The six basic steps in setup reduction are:

1. Measure the total setup time in the current state.
2. Identify the internal and external elements, calculating the individual times.
3. Convert as many of the internal elements to external as possible.
4. Reduce the time for the remaining internal elements.
5. Reduce the time for the external elements.
6. Standardize the new procedure.

*See:* Changeover, Single Minute Exchange of Die (SMED).


## Seven Wastes

Taiichi Ohno's categorization of the seven major wastes typically found in mass production:

1. **Overproduction**: Producing ahead of what's actually needed by the next process or customer. The worst form of waste because it contributes to the other six.

2. **Waiting**: Operators standing idle as machines cycle, equipment fails, needed parts fail to arrive, etc.

3. **Conveyance**: Moving parts and products unnecessarily, such as from a processing step to a warehouse to a subsequent processing step when the second step instead could be located immediately adjacent to the first step.

4. **Processing**: Performing unnecessary or incorrect processing, typically from poor tool or product design.

5. **Inventory**: Having more than the minimum stocks necessary for a precisely controlled pull system.

6. **Motion**: Operators making movements that are straining or unnecessary, such as looking for parts, tools, documents, etc.

7. **Correction**: Inspection, rework, and scrap.

*See:* Changeover, Setup Reduction.

## Shingo, Shigeo (1909–1990)

A consultant to Toyota who made key contributions to the understanding of the Toyota Production System, especially in quick changeovers.

The Shingo Prize for Excellence in Manufacturing was established in 1988 by the College of Business at Utah State University, to promote awareness of lean manufacturing concepts and recognizing private and public sector facilities in the United States, Canada, and Mexico that achieve high levels of implementation.

*See:* Setup Reduction, Single Minute Exchange of Die (SMED).

## Shojinka

One of three similar Japanese words (shojinka, shoninka, shoryokuka) related in concept but with different meanings. Shojinka means "flexible manpower line" and the ability to adjust the line to meet production requirements with any number of workers and demand changes. It is sometimes called "labor linearity" in English to refer to the capability of an assembly line to be balanced even when production volume fluctuates up or down.

Shoninka means "manpower savings." This corresponds to the improvement of work procedures, machines, or equipment, in order to free whole units of labor (i.e. one person) from a production line consisting of one or more workers.

Shoryokuka means "labor savings" and indicates partial improvement of manual labor by adding small machines or devices to aid the job. This results in some small amount of saved labor but not an entire person as in shoninka. (An accumulation of shoryokuka labor savings add up to shoninka manpower saving.)

*See:* Cell, Continuous Flow, Standardized Work.

## Shusa

*See:* Chief Engineer.

### Single Minute Exchange of Die (SMED)
A process for changing over production equipment from one part number to another in as little time as possible. SMED refers to the target of reducing changeover times to a single digit, or less than 10 minutes.

Shigeo Shingo's key insights about setup reduction, which were developed in the 1950s and 1960s, were separating internal setup operations—which can be done only when a machine is stopped (such as inserting a new die)—from external operations that can be performed while the machine is running (such as transporting the new die to the machine), and then converting internal setup operations to external operations. (Shingo 1985, p. 21–25.)

*See:* Changeover, Setup Reduction, Shingo.

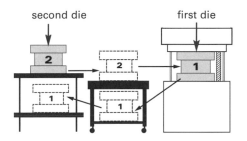

Slow changeover due to poor positioning of dies.

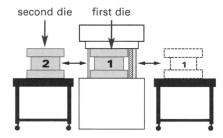

Quick changeover.

### Single-Piece Flow
*See:* Continuous Flow, One-Piece Flow.

### Six Sigma
A quality standard of just 3.4 defects per one million opportunities; 99.9996% perfect.

Six sigma methodologies emphasize mathematical and statistical tools to improve the quality of processes that are already under control. Application follows a five-step process of define, measure, analyze, improve, and control often referred to as DMAIC.

Motorola conceived the six sigma technique in 1986 as a way to achieve the company's improvement goals in manufacturing and support functions. The term refers to the number of standard deviations a point is away from the mean point in a bell curve. It often is represented as 6σ.

Many lean thinkers apply six sigma techniques to solve stubborn quality problems in value-adding processes that already are under control and where an analysis of the overall value-stream has eliminated nonvalue-adding processes.

*Compare*: Lean Thinking, Theory of Constraints (TOC).

## Spaghetti Chart
A diagram of the path taken by a product as it travels through the steps along a value stream. So called because in a mass production organization the product's route often looks like a plate of spaghetti.

*See:* Material Flow.

### Spaghetti Chart for Product Flows Along Value Streams

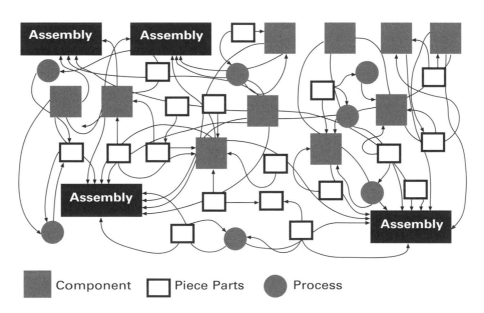

Component ☐ Piece Parts ● Process

## Standardized Work

Establishing precise procedures for each operator's work in a production process, based on three elements:

1. Takt time, which is the rate at which products must be made in a process to meet customer demand.

2. The precise work sequence in which an operator performs tasks within takt time.

3. The standard inventory, including units in machines, required to keep the process operating smoothly.

Standardized work, once established and displayed at workstations, is the object of continuous improvement through kaizen. The benefits of standardized work include documentation of the current process for all shifts, reductions in variability, easier training of new operators, reductions in injuries and strain, and a baseline for improvement activities.

Three basic forms (shown on the following pages) commonly are utilized in creating standardized work. These are used by engineers and front-line supervisors to design the process and by operators to make improvements in their own jobs.

### 1. Process Capacity Sheet

This form is used to calculate the capacity of each machine in a linked set of processes (often a cell) in order to confirm true capacity and to identify and eliminate bottlenecks. This form determines such factors as machine cycle times, tool setup and change intervals, and manual work times.

### 2. Standardized Work Combination Table

This form shows the combination of manual work time, walk time, and machine processing time for each operator in a production sequence. This form provides more detail and is a more precise process design tool than the *operator balance chart* (shown on page 54). The completed table shows the interactions between operators and machines in a process and permits the recalculation of operator work content as takt time expands and contracts over time.

| Process Capacity Sheet | Approved by: | Part # | | Application | | Entered by: |
|---|---|---|---|---|---|---|
| | | Part name | | Line | | |

| # | Process name | Machine # | BASIC TIME | | | TOOL CHANGE | | Processing capacity per shift |
|---|---|---|---|---|---|---|---|---|
| | | | MANUAL | AUTO | COMPLETION | CHANGE | TIME | |
| 1 | Cut | cc 100 | 5 | 25 | 30 | 500 | 2 min. | 896 |
| 2 | Rough Grind | gg 200 | 5 | 12 | 17 | 1000 | 5 min. | 1570 |
| 3 | Fine Grind | gg 300 | 5 | 27 | 32 | 300 | 5 min. | 823 |

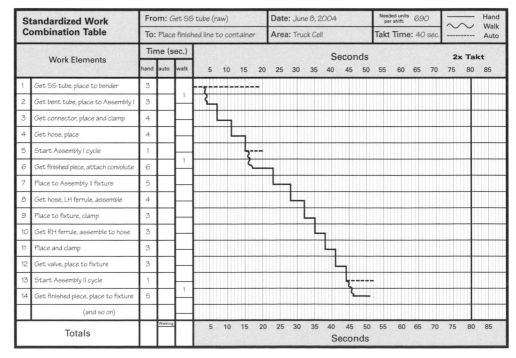

Standardized Work Combination Table — From: Get SS tube (raw); To: Place finished line to container; Date: June 8, 2004; Area: Truck Cell; Needed units per shift: 690; Takt Time: 40 sec.

| | Work Elements | hand | auto | walk |
|---|---|---|---|---|
| 1 | Get SS tube, place to bender | 3 | | 1 |
| 2 | Get bent tube, place to Assembly I | 3 | | |
| 3 | Get connector, place and clamp | 4 | | |
| 4 | Get hose, place | 4 | | |
| 5 | Start Assembly I cycle | 1 | | 1 |
| 6 | Get finished piece, attach convolute | 6 | | |
| 7 | Place to Assembly II fixture | 5 | | |
| 8 | Get hose, LH ferrule, assemble | 4 | | |
| 9 | Place to fixture, clamp | 3 | | |
| 10 | Get RH ferrule, assemble to hose | 3 | | |
| 11 | Place and clamp | 3 | | |
| 12 | Get valve, place to fixture | 3 | | |
| 13 | Start Assembly II cycle | 1 | | 1 |
| 14 | Get finished piece, place to fixture | 5 | | |
| | (and so on) | | | |

## 3. Standardized Work Chart

This form shows operator movement and material location in relation to the machine and overall process layout. The form should show the three elements that constitute standardized work: the current takt time (and cycle time) for the job, the work sequence, and the amount of required standard in-process stock to ensure smooth operations. Standardized work charts often are displayed at workstations as a tool for visual management and kaizen. They are continuously reviewed and updated as the condition of the worksite changes or improves.

These standardized work forms typically are used in conjunction with two other worksite forms: The *work standards sheet* and the *job instruction sheet*.

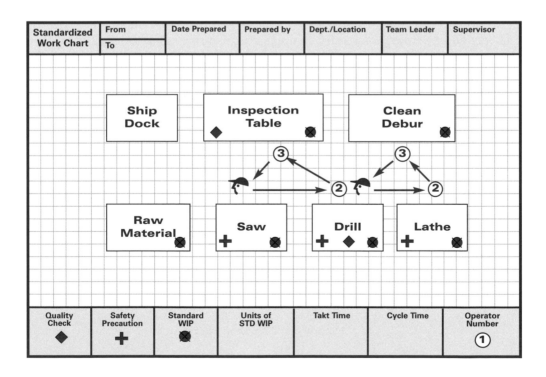

The work standards sheet summarizes a variety of documents that define how to build the product according to engineering specifications. Typically, the work standards sheet details precise operational requirements that must be adhered to in order to assure product quality.

The job instruction sheet—also called a *job breakdown sheet* or a *job element sheet*—is used to train new operators. The sheet lists the steps of the job, detailing any special knack that may be required to perform the job safely with utmost quality and efficiency.

*See:* Kaizen; Operator Balance Chart; Plan, Do, Check, Act (PDCA); Takt Time.


## Supermarket
The location where a predetermined standard inventory is kept to supply downstream processes.

Supermarkets ordinarily are located near the supplying process to help that process see customer usage and requirements. Each item in a supermarket has a specific location from which a material handler withdraws products in the precise amounts needed by a downstream process. As an item is removed, a signal to make more (such as a kanban card or an empty bin) is taken by the material handler to the supplying process.

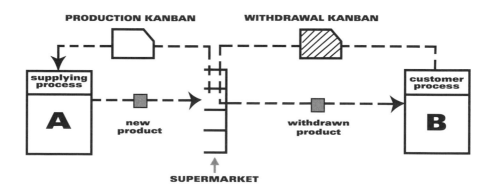

Diagram of a supermarket.

Toyota installed its first supermarket in 1953 in the machine shop of its main plant in Toyota City. (Ohno 1988, p. 27.) Toyota executive Taiichi Ohno took the idea for the supermarket from photos of American supermarkets showing goods arrayed on shelves by specific location for withdrawal by customers. (Ohno and Mito 1988, p. 16.)

*See:* Fill-Up System, Kanban, Material Handling, Pull System.


## Takt Image

Creating an awareness of takt time in areas of a production process where products cannot be delivered and taken away at the frequency of takt time.

On a final assembly line, takt time is easy to keep in mind because the line produces products at the rate of takt time. However, in upstream production cells and shared processes, such as stamping, a sense of takt time—which is the heartbeat of customer demand—may be hard to achieve.

Takt image often can be achieved by removing finished goods and delivering production signals at a multiple of takt time proportional to pack-out quantity or conveyance size. Thus a cell operating to a takt time of one minute that ships products downstream in pack sizes of 20 units would have a takt image of 20 minutes. While not as good as takt time, takt image still makes it possible to know within a few minutes if the process is out of step with customer demand.

*See:* Pitch, Takt Time.


## Takt Time

The available production time divided by customer demand.

For example, if a widget factory operates 480 minutes per day and customers demand 240 widgets per day, takt time is two minutes. Similarly, if customers want two new products per month, takt time is two weeks. The purpose of takt time is to precisely match production with demand. It provides the heartbeat of a lean production system.

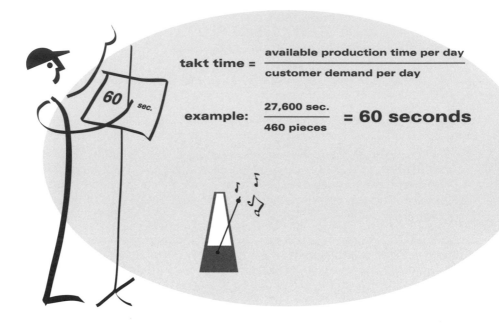

$$\text{takt time} = \frac{\text{available production time per day}}{\text{customer demand per day}}$$

$$\text{example:} \quad \frac{27{,}600 \text{ sec.}}{460 \text{ pieces}} = \textbf{60 seconds}$$

Takt time first was used as a production management tool in the German aircraft industry in the 1930s. (Takt is German for a precise interval of time such as a musical meter.) It was the interval at which aircraft were moved ahead to the next production station. The concept was widely utilized within Toyota in the 1950s and was in widespread use throughout the Toyota supply base by the late 1960s. Toyota typically reviews the takt time for a process every month, with a tweaking review every 10 days.

*See:* Cycle Time, Heijunka, Just-in-Time, Operator Balance Chart, Pacemaker Process, Pitch, Takt Image.

### Target Cost

The development and production cost that a product cannot exceed if the customer is to be satisfied with the value of the product while the manufacturer obtains an acceptable return on its investment.

Toyota developed target costing for its small supplier group with which it has had long-term relations. Because there is no market price available from taking bids or conducting an auction, Toyota and its suppliers determine a correct/fair cost (and price) for a supplied item by estimating what the customer thinks the item is worth and then working backwards to take out cost (waste) to meet the price while preserving Toyota and supplier profit margins.

## Team Leader

At Toyota, an hourly worker who leads a team of five to eight other workers; called hancho in Japanese.

Team leaders in the Toyota Production System form the first line of support for workers, who—unlike their counterparts in traditional mass production organizations—are at the heart of improvement activities with responsibility for problem solving, quality assurance, and basic preventive maintenance.

Team leaders do not take disciplinary action and do not have a fixed production job. Rather, they provide support by knowing all the jobs performed by their team members so they can relieve workers, fill in for absentees, or help workers who need assistance or are falling behind. They respond to problems such as line stops, andon calls, and take a lead role in kaizen activities. They also use standardized work audit sheets to do daily checks of team members to make sure people are following standardized work and to surface problems.

*See*: Andon, Group Leader, Preventive Maintenance, Standardized Work, Toyota Production System.

## Theory of Constraints (TOC)

A management philosophy and a set of tools for organizational change developed by Israeli physicist Dr. Eliyahu Goldratt and popularized in the 1984 book *The Goal* by Goldratt and Jeff Cox. TOC concentrates on improving profits by managing constraints, factors that prevent a company from achieving its goals. Its primary focus is on removing or managing constraints to improve throughput, while lean focuses on the identification and removal of waste to improve the flow of value. Both lean and TOC emphasize improving the whole system rather than individual parts.

*Compare*: Lean Thinking, Six Sigma.

**Three Ms**
*See:* Muda, Mura, Muri.


**Three Ps**
*See:* Production Preparation Process.


**Throughput Time**
*See:* Cycle Time.


**Total Productive Maintenance (TPM)**

A set of techniques, originally pioneered by Denso in the Toyota Group in Japan, to ensure that every machine in a production process always is able to perform its required tasks.

The approach is termed *total* in three senses. First, it requires the total participation of all employees, not only maintenance personnel but line managers, manufacturing engineers, quality experts, and operators. Second, it seeks total productivity of equipment by focusing on all of the six major losses that plague equipment: downtime, changeover time, minor stops, speed losses, scrap, and rework. Third, it addresses the total life cycle of equipment to revise maintenance practices, activities, and improvements in relation to where equipment is in its life cycle.

Unlike traditional preventive maintenance, which relies on maintenance personnel, TPM involves operators in routine maintenance, improvement projects, and simple repairs. For example, operators perform daily activities such as lubricating, cleaning, tightening, and inspecting equipment.

*See:* Overall Equipment Effectiveness (OEE).


**Total Quality Control (TQC)**

A management approach in which all departments, employees, and managers are responsible for continuously improving quality so that products and services meet or exceed customer expectations.

The TQC methodology relies on the plan-do-check-act (PDCA) cycle to manage processes and, when problems arise, statistical tools to solve them. The methodology and tools are used often by employees during kaizen activities and together form an important subsystem of lean.

The term "total quality control" was coined in 1957 by U.S. quality expert Armand Feigenbaum, who saw quality control professionals as central to promoting TQC. By the 1980s, other experts such as Philip Crosby, Joseph Juran, W. Edwards Deming, and Kaoru Ishikawa expanded the concept, now known as Total Quality Management, to include new tools and, most importantly, the idea that quality was the responsibility of all employees, managers, and senior managers.

Toyota implemented TQC in the early 1960s and began transferring the system to suppliers in the late 1960s.

*See*: Plan Do Check Act, Toyota Production System.


## Total Quality Management
*See*: Total Quality Control.


## Toyoda, Kiichiro (1894–1952)
The son of Toyota Group founder Sakichi Toyoda, who led the effort to enter the auto industry in the 1930s. Kiichiro believed that he could keep the entire production process stocked with needed goods if the preceding process would simply respond to the precise needs of the next downstream process. He called this system just-in-time, which became one of the two pillars of the Toyota Production System.

*See:* Toyoda, Sakichi; Toyota Production System.


## Toyoda, Sakichi (1867–1930)
The founder of the Toyota Group, who invented a self-monitoring device for textile looms in the early 1900s that stopped the loom if a thread broke. This innovation allowed one operator to tend multiple machines and led to the concept of jidoka, which means "automation with human intelligence." It is one of the two pillars of the Toyota Production System.

*See:* Toyoda, Kiichiro; Toyota Production System.

## Toyota Production System (TPS)

The production system developed by Toyota Motor Corporation to provide best quality, lowest cost, and shortest lead time through the elimination of waste. TPS is comprised of two pillars, just-in-time and jidoka, and often is illustrated with the "house" shown at right. TPS is maintained and improved through iterations of standardized work and kaizen, following PDCA, or the scientific method.

Development of TPS is credited to Taiichi Ohno, Toyota's chief of production in the post-WW II period. Beginning in machining operations and spreading from there, Ohno led the development of TPS at Toyota throughout the 1950s and 1960s, and the dissemination to the supply base through the 1960s and 1970s. Outside Japan, dissemination began in earnest with the creation of the Toyota-General Motors joint venture—NUMMI—in California in 1984.

The concepts of just-in-time (JIT) and jidoka both have their roots in the prewar period. Sakichi Toyoda, founder of the Toyota group of companies, invented the concept of jidoka in the early 20th Century

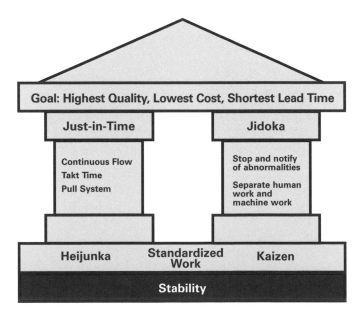

Toyota Production System "House."

by incorporating a device on his automatic looms that would stop the loom from operating whenever a thread broke. This enabled great improvements in quality and freed people to do more value-creating work than simply monitoring machines for quality. Eventually, this simple concept found its way into every machine, every production line, and every Toyota operation.

Kiichiro Toyoda, son of Sakichi and founder of the Toyota automobile business, developed the concept of JIT in the 1930s. He decreed that Toyota operations would contain no excess inventory and that Toyota would strive to work in partnership with suppliers to level production. Under Ohno's leadership, JIT developed into a unique system of material and information flows to control overproduction.

Widespread recognition of TPS as the model production system grew rapidly with the publication in 1990 of *The Machine That Changed the World*, the result of five years of research led by the Massachusetts Institute of Technology. The MIT researchers found that TPS was so much more effective and efficient than traditional mass production that it represented a completely new paradigm and coined the term *lean production* to indicate this radically different approach to production.

*See:* Jidoka; Just-in-Time; Lean Production; Ohno, Taiichi; Toyoda, Kiichiro; Toyoda, Sakichi.


## Tsurube System

A method for maintaining flow between decoupled processes. Such processes may be separated due to a step outside the line or plant that is too expensive or too big to move. Using a pull-FIFO technique, tsurube maintains a standard number of parts exiting and returning to the system in sequential order. Tsurube houshiki is the Japanese term for a two-bucket system of drawing water from a well: one empty bucket goes down for water while a full one — attached to the same rope running through a pulley — comes to the top.

In the example, which shows part of a value stream, a tsurube system maintains flow between the main process and heat treatment. Every 20 minutes a set number of items arrive at the heat treatment FIFO lane from the FIFO lane after operation 20.

Also every 20 minutes, the same number of treated items are transported from the FIFO lane after heat treatment to the FIFO lane for the next step, operation 40. The FIFO lanes maintain the sequence of items to be processed. (The solid blue arrows show material flow through the processes.) Because of the paced delivery and withdrawal, managers will know in 20 minutes if there is any disruption. To improve the system, managers would ask why heat treatment is isolated and how it could be coupled with the system. Having stable manufacturing processes is a precondition for implementing a tsurube system in order to maintain flow and pull production.

*See:* Continuous Flow; First In, First Out (FIFO); Pull Production.

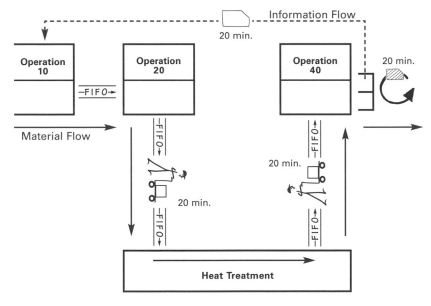

Example of a tsurube system.

## Value

The inherent worth of a product as judged by the customer and reflected in its selling price and market demand.

The value in a typical product is created by the producer through a combination of actions, some of which produce value as perceived by the customers and some of which are merely necessary given the current configuration of the design and production process. The objective of Lean Thinking is to eliminate the latter class of activities while preserving or enhancing the first set.

**Value-Creating**
Any activity that the customer judges of value. A simple test as to whether a task and its time is value-creating is to ask if the customer would judge a product less valuable if this task could be left out without affecting the product. For example, rework and queue time are unlikely to be judged of any value by customers, while actual design and fabrication steps are.

**Nonvalue-Creating**
Any activity that adds cost but no value to the product or service as seen through the eyes of the customer.

## Value-Creating Time
*See:* Cycle Time.

## Value Stream
All of the actions, both value-creating and nonvalue-creating, required to bring a product from concept to launch and from order to delivery. These include actions to process information from the customer and actions to transform the product on its way to the customer.

## Value-Stream Manager
An individual assigned clear responsibility for the success of a value stream. The value stream may be defined on the product or business level (including product development) or on the plant or operations level (from raw materials to delivery). The value-stream manager is the architect of the value stream, identifying value as defined from the customer's perspective and leading the effort to achieve an ever-shortening value-creating flow.

The value-stream manager focuses the organization on aligning activities and resources around value creation, though none of the resources (money, assets, people) may actually "belong to" the value-stream manager. Thus, value-stream management distinguishes between responsibility, which resides with the value-stream manager, and authority, which may reside inside functions and departments holding the resources. The role of the functions is to provide the resources needed to achieve the value-stream vision, as defined by the value-stream manager. The value-stream manager leads through influence, not position, and thus can be equally effective in a traditional functional organization or in a matrix organization, avoiding the common failure of matrix organizations, which is the loss of clear responsibility, accountability, and effective decision-making.

The archetype for the role of the value-stream manager is the Toyota chief engineer, who has only minimal staff and resources under his direct control.

*See:* Chief Engineer.

## Value-Stream Mapping (VSM)
A simple diagram of every step involved in the material and information flows needed to bring a product from order to delivery.

Value-stream maps can be drawn for different points in time as a way to raise consciousness of opportunities for improvement. A current-state map, shown upper right, follows a product's path from order to delivery to determine the current conditions.

A future-state map, shown lower right, deploys the opportunities for improvement identified in the current-state map to achieve a higher level of performance at some future point.

In some cases, it may be appropriate to draw an ideal-state map showing the opportunities for improvement by employing all known lean methods including right-sized tools and value-stream compression.

*See:* Information Flow, Material Flow.

## Current-State Value-Stream Map

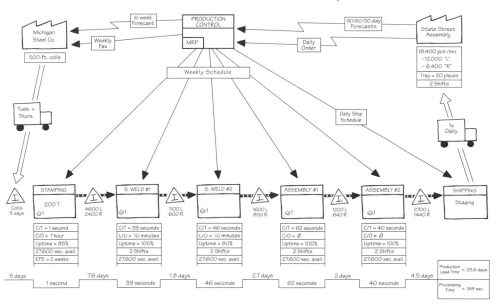

## Future-State Value-Stream Map

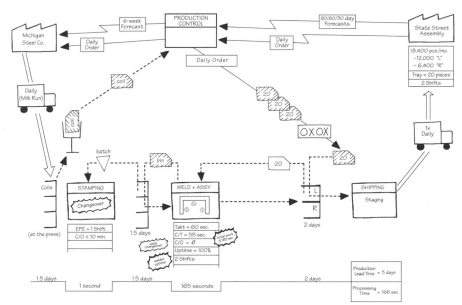

Source: Rother and Shook 1999, pp. 32–33 and 78–79.

## Visual Management

The placement in plain view of all tools, parts, production activities, and indicators of production system performance, so the status of the system can be understood at a glance by everyone involved.

*See:* Andon, Jidoka.


## Waste

Any activity that consumes resources but creates no value for the customer. Most activities are waste—muda—and fall into one of two types. *Type one muda* creates no value but is unavoidable with current technologies and production assets. An example would be inspecting welds to ensure they are safe.

*Type two muda* creates no value and can be eliminated immediately. An example is a process with disconnected steps in process villages that can be quickly reconfigured into a cell where wasteful materials movements and inventories no longer are required.

Most value-stream activities that actually create value as perceived by the customer are a tiny fraction of the total activities. Eliminating the large number of wasteful activities is the greatest potential source of improvement in corporate performance and customer service.

*See:* Muda, Seven Wastes.


## Waterspider
*See:* Material Handling.


## Work Element

The distinct steps required to complete one cycle at a workstation; the smallest increment of work that can be moved to another operator.

Breaking work into its elements helps to identify and eliminate waste that is hidden within an operator's cycle. The elements can be distributed in relation to takt time to create continuous flow. For instance, in the Operator Balance Chart on p. 60 the small vertical boxes represent work elements.

*See*: Operator Balance Chart.

### Work-in-Process (WIP)
*See:* Inventory.


### Work
Human actions (motions) involved in producing products. These actions can be divided into three categories:

1. **Value-Creating**: Movements directly necessary for making products, such as welding, drilling, and painting.

2. **Incidental Work**: Motions that operators must perform to make products but that do not create value from the standpoint of the customer, such as reaching for a tool or clamping a fixture.

3. **Waste**: Motions that create no value and can be eliminated, such as walking to get parts or tools that could be positioned within reach.

## Categories of Work Motion Diagram

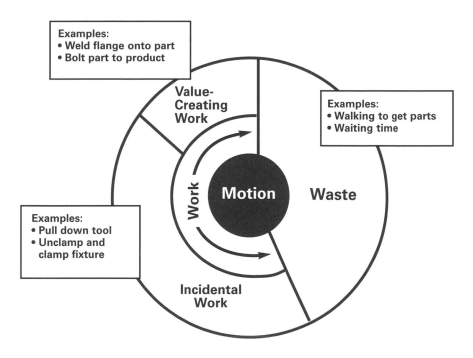

## Yamazumi Board
Yamazumi is Japanese for "pile" or "stack."

*See:* Operator Balance Chart.


## Yokoten
A Japanese term for deploying concepts, ideas, or policies horizontally across the company.

For example, imagine a defective valve is found on one machine in the plant. Yokoten would be the process to ensure that all similar valves in the facility and other relevant facilities are examined for the same defect as well.

*See*: Catchball.

| Material Icons | Represent | Notes |
|---|---|---|
| ASSEMBLY | Process | One process box equals an area of flow. All processes should be labeled. Also used for departments, such as Production Control. |
| XYZ Corporation | Outside Sources | Used to show customers, suppliers, and outside manufacturing processes. |
| C/T = 45 sec. <br> C/O = 30 min. <br> 3 Shifts <br> 2% Scrap | Data Box | Used to record information concerning a manufacturing process, department, customer, etc. |
| (cross-dock icon) | Cross-Dock | Materials are not stored but rather moved from in-bound trucks to shipping lanes for out-bound trucks. |
| (warehouse icon) | Warehouse | Materials are placed in storage locations (binned) and then picked for out-bound shipment at some later point. |
| (plane icon) 2x year | Plane Shipment | Note frequency of shipments. |
| (train icon) 1x day | Train Shipment | Note frequency of shipments. |
| (truck icon) Mon. + Wed. | Truck Shipment | Note frequency of shipments. |
| (boat icon) 1x month | Boat Shipment | Note frequency of shipments. |

| Material Icons | Represent | Notes |
|---|---|---|
| (triangle with I) **300 pcs. 1 Day** | Inventory | Count and time should be noted. |
| (striped arrow) | Movement of production material by pushing. | Material that is produced and moved forward before the next process needs it; usually based on a schedule. |
| (open arrow) | Movement of finished goods to the customer. | |
| (loop arrow) | Milk Run | |
| (dotted arrow) | Expedited Transport | |
| (bracket) | Supermarket | A controlled inventory of parts that is used to schedule production at an upstream process. The open side faces the supplying process. |
| (circular arrow) | Withdrawal | Pull of materials, usually from a supermarket. |
| **max. 20 pcs.** **−FIFO→** | Transfer of controlled quantities of material between processes in a first-in, first-out sequence. | Indicates a method to limit quantity and ensure FIFO flow of material between processes. Maximum quantity should be noted. |
| (stacked boxes) | Buffer or Safety Stock | "Buffer" or "safety stock" must be noted. |

| Information Icons | Represent | Notes |
|---|---|---|
| ◄─────────── | Manual Information Flow | For example, production or shipping schedule. |
| ◄───╱╲─── | Electronic Information Flow | For example, via electronic data interchange. |
| Weekly Schedule | Information | Describes an information flow. |
| ◄ - 20 - - - | Production Kanban (dotted line indicates kanban path) | The "one-per-container" kanban. Card or device that tells a process how many of what can be produced and gives permission to do so. |
| ◄ - ▨ - - - | Withdrawal Kanban | Card or device that instructs the material handler to get and transfer parts (i.e., from a supermarket to the consuming process). |
| ◄ - ▽ - - - | Signal Kanban | The "one-per-batch" kanban signals when a reorder point is reached and another batch needs to be produced. Used where supplying process must produce in batches because changeovers are required. |
| ⊔ | Kanban Post or Collection Box | Place where kanban are collected and held for conveyance. |
| ◄ - ⬠ - - | Kanban Arriving in Batches | |
| OXOX | Load Leveling | Tool to intercept batches of kanban and level the volume and mix of them over a period of time. |

| Information Icons | Represent | Notes |
|---|---|---|
| | Control Center | Often a computerized system such as a Material Requirements Planning system. |
| | Phone | Usually for expedited information. |
| | Orders | Often in electronic form. |

**General Icons**

| | Operator | Represents a person viewed from above. |
|---|---|---|
| weld changeover / welder uptime | Kaizen Lightning Bursts | Highlights improvement needs on a value-stream map at specific processes that are critical to achieving the value-stream vision; can be used to plan kaizen workshops. |
| | Go-See Scheduling | Adjusts schedules based on checking inventory levels. |

## Lean Acronyms Referred to in This Lexicon

3M—Muda, Mura, Muri

3P—Production Preparation Process

4M—Material, Machine, Man, Method

5S—Sort, Straighten, Shine, Standardize, Sustain

EPEx—Every Product Every Interval

FIFO—First In, First Out

JIT—Just-in-Time

OBC—Operator Balance Chart

OEE—Overall Equipment Effectiveness

PDCA—Plan, Do, Check, Act

PFEP—Plan For Every Part

SMED—Single Minute Exchange of Die

TPM—Total Productive Maintenance

TPS—Toyota Production System

WIP—Work-in-Process

VSM—Value-Stream Mapping

## Lean Terms of Japanese Origin in This Lexicon

| | |
|---|---|
| Andon | Seiketsu |
| Baka-Yoke | Seiri |
| Chaku-Chaku | Seiso |
| Gemba | Seiton |
| Genchi Genbutsu | Sensei |
| Hansei | Shitsuke |
| Heijunka | Shojinka |
| Hoshin Kanri | Shusa |
| Jidoka | Tsurube |
| Jishuken | Yamazumi |
| Kaikaku | Yokoten |
| Kaizen | |
| Kanban | |
| Mizusumashi | |
| Muda | |
| Mura | |
| Muri | |
| Nemawashi | |
| Obeya | |
| Poka-Yoke | |

## Lean Terms of German Origin in This Lexicon

Takt

## Pronunciation Guide to Japanese Words

Here is a simple pronunciation guide to the Japanese terms in the *Lean Lexicon*:

1. All syllables end in a vowel. (Almost all, a few exceptions end in *N*.)

2. All vowels are pronounced the same, every time. Simple vowels only, no diphthongs.

3. The only consonant that is really problematic is the letter *R*, which is trilled once. (This is similar to the trill of a Spanish or Italian *R*, although those languages usually trill *R*s twice.)

The five Japanese vowels are:

A = "ah" as in "c**a**r", not "c**a**n"
I  = "ee" as in "id**i**ot", not "**i**diot"
U = "ooh" as in "st**u**pid", not "d**u**mb"
E = "eh" as in "b**e**t", not "b**e**at"
O = "oh" as in "n**o**", not "n**o**t"

Vowels combined may be pronounced:

**A + I** together, as in "hai" sounds like "hi" or "high."
**E + I** together with an H in front (hei) sounds like "hey" or "hay."

So, for example, the correct pronunciations are:

Kanban = Kahn-bahn
Pokayoke = Poh-kah-yoh-kay
Jidoka = Jee-doh-kah
Heijunka = Hey-joon-kah
Kaizen = Kai-zen

Do not make plurals of Japanese terms in English: *two* kanban; not *two kanbans*.

## Cited Works

Harris, Rick; Harris, Chris; Wilson, Earl, 2003. *Making Materials Flow*. Cambridge, MA: Lean Enterprise Institute.

Ohno, Taiichi, 1988. *Toyota Production System*. New York: Productivity Press.

Ohno, Taiichi, and Mito, Setsuo, 1988. *Just-in-Time for Today and Tomorrow*. New York: Productivity Press.

Rother, Mike, and Harris, Rick, 2001. *Creating Continuous Flow*. Cambridge, MA: Lean Enterprise Institute.

Rother, Mike, and Shook, John, 1998. *Learning to See*. Cambridge, MA: Lean Enterprise Institute.

Shingo, Shigeo, 1985. *A Revolution in Manufacturing: The SMED System*. New York: Productivity Press.

Smalley, Art, 2004. *Creating Level Pull*. Cambridge, MA: Lean Enterprise Institute.

Toyota Motor Corporation, 1995. *The Toyota Production System*, Toyota City, Japan: International Public Affairs Division, Operations Management Consulting Division.

Womack, James, and Jones, Daniel, 1996. *Lean Thinking*. New York: Simon & Schuster.

Womack, James, and Jones, Daniel, 2005. *Lean Solutions*. New York: Simon & Schuster.

Womack, James, and Jones, Daniel, 2002. *Seeing the Whole: Mapping the Extended Value Stream*. Cambridge, MA: Lean Enterprise Institute.

Womack, James; Jones, Daniel; Roos, Daniel, 1990. *The Machine That Changed the World*. New York: Rawson Associates.